M-ROD

A Way Out

**faith, hope and the love
of the game**

BILLY WAGNER

with Patty Rasmussen

ampelōn
PUBLISHING

ISBN: 978-0-9893419-0-5
First Edition 2013

Printed in the United States of America
Requests for information should be addressed to:
Ampelon Publishing
PO Box 140675
Boise, ID 83714

To order other Ampelon Publishing products, visit us on the web at:
www.ampelonpublishing.com

Cover & inside design: Jared Swafford — SwingFromTheRafters.com
Cover photos by Sam Dean — samdeanphotography.com
Wagner family photo by Donna Marie Fine Art Photography
Astros photos courtesy of the Houston Astros
Phillies photos courtesy of the Philadelphia Phillies
Mets photos courtesy of the New York Mets

Printed on paper and with ink made from sustainable resources

*This book is dedicated to all the people
who gave me time and support,
a pat on the back or a boot in the butt.*

CONTENTS

ACKNOWLEDGMENTS

I want to thank my publisher, Jason Chatraw, at Ampelon Publishing. Jason heard my story early on in the process and thought it had potential and value. He believed in it when others didn't. Thanks to my editor David Jacobsen who went through the manuscript and did a great job of streamlining the story, making sure it made sense and the message didn't get lost.

Thank you to Patty Rasmussen for helping put my thoughts into a book. I knew what I wanted to say, but I couldn't have put it in any sort of readable form without her. She listened to me, asked questions, got what I was feeling and trying to express and put it on paper.

Teammates, coaches and managers were very influential in my life and many are mentioned in the book. There were other people that came into my life at different times, sometimes just for a quick conversation, but they impacted me. To be honest with you, there are just too many to name and if I tried, I know I'd forget someone.

Many guys reached out in friendship and concern for no other reason than they wanted me to be not just successful, but happy and content; they acted out of pure selflessness. I believe God put these men in my life to keep me grounded, to keep me focused, to keep me humble. I felt the impact of their words at the time and I still feel them today. They helped me become the man I've become. You guys know who you are and I appreciate each of you.

Thank you to my cousin, Jeff Lamie, for being a great motivator to me. He was a huge influence; wasn't vocal but he set a great example. I worked hard because I wanted to be like him. Not only was he someone I looked up to, but his actions, talking to his parents about me moving in with their family, changed the course of my life. His willingness to speak up for me allowed me to become who I am.

I can't thank my wife, Sarah, enough for what she's done for me and what she means to me. Everything we went through together brought us closer, helped us to understand each other better and, in Sarah's case, helped her to overlook things that I'm sure she didn't like about me. She has supported me with love as I went through my career, and the appreciation I have for her has only increased since I retired and realized all the things she does every day to keep the Wagner family on track. My life is busier now than when I played baseball. I go in more directions, but Sarah's love and support is always there.

I appreciate the fans who watched me during my baseball career. Whether you cheered for me or booed me, I hope you know I gave it my all when I was on the mound. And thank you for buying my book. I've been blessed in many ways, especially financially. The proceeds I earn from this book will go to various charities and scholarships for kids.

Writing this book has given me the chance to look at how far I've come, who I was and what I'm becoming. This process has made me realize more than ever that the down times, not the times on the mountaintops, made me who I am. Looking back on your life is a humbling experience, but it was worthwhile because I think there is value in the lessons my life has taught.

There's more at work here than just a baseball story. I'm not telling the story of my life to talk about me. This book is a lot like coaching, bringing my experiences to another person, a kid, and trying to make a difference. I want my life to mean something and I don't want it to mean something solely through a baseball experience. Baseball is my platform; it's not my message. It's not who I am. God used baseball to give me a voice.

It's a cliché but I give my heartfelt thanks to God for every blessing and every challenge He sent my way. I thank Him for loving me and giving me a chance to let everyone know how much I love and honor Him.

Billy Wagner
Nonesuch Farm
Crozet, Virginia
January 2013

* * *

First and foremost, I thank God for more blessings than I can count. He makes all things possible and I am grateful for His infinite mercy and grace.

Thank you to Billy who said "yes" to this idea of writing a book. From the beginning we had a shared vision of what we hoped this book could be. We believed that, just as God had a plan for Billy's life, He also had a plan for us meeting during the 2010 season. Billy and I believe that there was simply no other way to tell his story except through the lens of his faith. We would not have wanted to tell it any other way.

Thank you to Jason Chatraw who believed in this project when I first brought it to him to the point that he said, "I'll publish it myself," and to David Jacobsen for his skilled editing.

Thank you to Gary Caruso, Susan Percy, Jack Wilkinson and Carroll Rogers, excellent editors and writers (and friends) from whom I've learned so much, and to Steve Copses who gave me a break.

Thank you to my parents, my siblings and their spouses and my friends, especially those in my Small Group. I can't thank them enough for the prayers, encouragement and love they've given me over the years. Special thanks go to my children Matt and Jenny, Tim, Joanna, granddaughters Elena and Annika and my husband, Steve, who believed in me before I believed in myself.

Patty Rasmussen
Conyers, Georgia
January 2013

FOREWORD
by Lance Berkman

ON JULY 25, 1999, I found myself standing in left field in the Astrodome in a game against the Arizona Diamondbacks. I had just been called up to the big leagues a week earlier and, needless to say, I was still experiencing rookie jitters. To make matters worse, the D-backs had the bases loaded in the eighth inning of a one-run game and two outs. Into this tense situation trotted our closer Billy Wagner to face pesky leadoff man Tony Womack. With the outcome of the game riding on this confrontation, the last place I wanted the ball hit was to me! Of course, as anyone with experience in the game knows, the minute you think that, the ball will invariably be hit to you. Sure enough, Billy threw a pitch high and tight, but Womack made just enough contact to send a looping liner out toward me in left field. I got a good jump on the ball and felt like I had a bead on it, but it was going to be close.

I had been around Billy a few times after I signed with the Astros in 1997, but I really got to know him during offseason workouts at the Astrodome. It was a big deal for me to get to workout at the dome, as I was still in the minor leagues and the Astros generally reserved their offseason workouts at the stadium for their major league players. The first day I walked in, Astros strength coach Gene Colman paired me with Billy and told me, "Try to keep up." He wasn't kidding. Billy attacked our workouts like a man possessed. That's one of the first things that impressed me about him. He is a man that is wholehearted in what he endeavors to do. Full speed ahead!

He was also great to me. He treated me like I was already in the big leagues even though I hadn't accomplished anything in professional baseball yet. That's another quality of Billy's that I admire. You could be a king or a bum off the street and Billy would treat you with the same kindness and consideration. As a young player, I was encouraged that someone of Billy's stature would take the time to show me how major leaguers go about their business.

Another great trait about Billy is you always know where you stand with him. If he's upset with you or pleased, he'll tell you exactly that. If he says something, he means it. It's refreshing in today's world of image maintenance to find a public figure unafraid to present the unvarnished truth. It might not always be pretty or what you want to hear but Billy will shoot you straight!

Back to the game. About halfway to the ball I knew I was going to have to dive to have a chance of catching it. As I prepared to launch myself to make the catch, the ball seemed to die and started sinking fast. I knew I was in trouble. I came up about a foot short as the ball bounded into the left field corner. Though I hustled after the ball, Womack was faster. He circled the bases and I realized that I had just allowed an inside-the-park grand slam, as well as costing our team any chance of winning the game. I felt more pain inside than I did from the artificial turf burn I suffered on my forearm from the ill-fated dive. I was embarrassed and didn't even want to run back to the dugout after the anticlimactic third out was recorded. When I did get back, the first person to greet me was Billy. He put his arm around me and told me he was proud of my effort and not to worry that I hadn't made the play. He said he would rather have someone behind him that would go all out for a ball than to play it safe. His words of encouragement were just what I needed to hear as a young player. Instead of being focused on the runs he just gave up and what that would do to his statistics, he was concerned about me. That's a great teammate and the kind of heart that is pleasing to the Lord.

There is one more thing that stands out to me about Billy. He is so real. There is no pretense about the man. His journey of faith with the Lord is the same way. It's wholehearted and honest—and like any journey fraught with difficulties to be overcome. Billy will be the first to tell you that he's not perfect and it hasn't always been easy, but God is looking for people who are willing to learn from their mistakes and carry on. He wants big hearted and courageous people to carry His message of love and reconciliation to a hurting world. Billy is the type of person that God has used and will continue to use to accomplish His purposes. I hope that this book will inspire and encourage you as Billy has done for me and many others.

Lance Berkman
St. Louis, July 2012

CHAPTER ONE

FINAL GAME, FINAL SAVE

THE FINAL WEEK of my sixteen year baseball career was a jumble of emotions: excitement, fear, doubt, joy, disbelief, sadness, and nostalgia. And deeper than all those was another emotion: satisfaction. I'd reached the culmination of a lifetime of overcoming obstacles and trusting God, and I knew it was time to hang up my glove for good.

I chose to retire because it was time to stop putting my career first and start focusing on the family God had given me. A year later, as I handled carpool duties, coached my sons, watched my daughter dance at a recital, and took my wife out to her favorite restaurant, I knew in my heart that I'd made the right choice.

That doesn't mean it was easy to drive away from Turner Field for the last time after our final playoff game in 2010. I watched the stadium shrink in my rearview mirror. I thought about all the things I'd never do again: put on my 'uni' and lace up my spikes, hear my entrance music blaring from the stadium speakers, or step onto the mound as the crowd roared. I'd never become Billy the Kid again. It was the right choice, but I was still turning my back on what had consumed my adult life.

When a dream takes a long time to achieve, sometimes you're too focused on getting there to appreciate the journey and have fun along the way. My first two years in the bigs were fun. Back then it was just me and Sarah and the joy of playing the game. Before long I was either thinking about the next game or the next house payment. The feeling of being in the moment, savoring the brightly-lit stage of the pitcher's mound, got lost in the shuffle.

In April 2010, with most of the season still ahead of me, I realized it was time to have fun again. It was time to retire from professional baseball at the end of the season.

So after that final week, as Turner Field disappeared behind me, I thought, *There's nothing left for me to do in baseball. I'm not going to change anyone's mind about whether I'm a Hall of Famer. People are either going to like me or hate me, and I can't change their minds. Besides, life's about a lot more than this game...*

I was leaving the game with 422 saves, only two shy of John Franco's all-time record for left-handed relievers. I knew that if not for injuries I would have passed that mark, but as I drove away I said to myself, *I'm content. I'm content with that.* Whether my name was at the top of some page in a record book had no bearing on who I really was—or even on what I'd come to realize was most important to me.

My family trumped anything I did or could accomplish on the baseball field. I remember hearing my pastor preach on 1 Corinthians 13:11 one time. It says, "When I was a child, I used to speak like a child, think like a child, and reason like a child; when I became a man, I did away with childish things."

Retirement was doing away with childish things. I'm not taking away from the game when I say that. Baseball gave me an opportunity to support my family and the causes that matter to us. But playing took me away from the most important thing in my life. The tradeoff was too high. So as I drove away that final time, I had no regrets. My children would know me as their dad instead of some guy who played baseball long past when he should have stopped.

God used baseball to teach me things I wouldn't have understood any other way. I learned how to trust Him with absolutely everything—success, fame, disappointment, my teammates, money, how I used my time, and how I conducted myself. Baseball was God's classroom for me, and without the mistakes I made—and there were a lot, as you'll see!—I wouldn't be as thankful or humble or convinced that God's plans are always the best plans. When I was a kid growing up dirt-poor in rural Virginia, I never suspected what might be on the road ahead.

God knew. He knew my heart and what made me tick. He knew He could teach me, through adversity and competition and pressure, to trust Him. And He knew exactly when to call me up to the next stage of my life.

Before I can tell you where I came from or what I learned, though, I want to tell you about my final games...

THE FINAL SAVE

The last regular season game of 2010 was one of the most exciting of my 16-year career—and I've played in plenty of exciting games. It was October 3, 2010, and I was called in to win a vital game for the Atlanta Braves. We'd swept the Florida Marlins in a three game series the week before, only to lose the first two games of the final weekend series with the Philadelphia Phillies. Sunday morning we found ourselves tied with the Padres for the National League Wild Card. To get into the playoffs we'd need to win the final game against the Phils—and then pray the San Francisco Giants beat the San Diego Padres later that day so we wouldn't need to play a one-game tie-breaker against the Padres.

I'd announced my retirement in April, so everyone knew this could be my last game. It could be Bobby Cox's last game, too, and we wanted to play our hearts out for our legendary manager.

Confession time for this All-Star relief pitcher: I'm a nervous person with a terrible fear of failure. After sixteen years I still got nervous when I went in to close out games—heart in my throat, about to puke. I didn't know it when the game started that October morning, but it was going to be one of the most nerve wracking experiences of my life.

That's why I want to tell you about it, because it's a perfect example of how God took a kid from the sticks in southwest Virginia and plunked him down on a pitcher's mound in front of thousands of fans. He took a kid that schoolteachers said would never amount to anything and gave him a career, a loving family, financial security, and the ability to give back to others. He took an angry, hurt kid and grew him into a man who could choose to love and forgive the people who had hurt him most. Where others saw weakness, God saw strength—and the last game of the 2010 season was only the latest example of that.

The Phillies were one of my favorite teams because they had great players who loved to compete. That brought out my best. I loved pitching against guys like Chase Utley and Jimmy Rollins because if I made a mistake they would make me pay. I'd rather get beat by the best than beat by the worst.

But *that* day I didn't want to get beat at all.

We had an afternoon start with perfect weather. It was sunny and clear, but by the time I entered the game the shadows could be a factor...for the hitters. Our fans were out in force. Turner Field was packed with over 50,000 fans who had come to cheer their Braves into the playoffs or else say farewell to Bobby Cox.

Thanks to solid pitching from Tim Hudson and good hitting in the middle innings, the game looked pretty well in hand; we led 8-4 in the seventh inning. Our young relief pitcher, Jonny Venters, replaced Hudson in the top of the eighth, but after getting two outs things got away from him. I got the call with men on the corners and two outs.

My fiery clip from the movie "Tombstone" flashed on the Jumbotron as the opening riff from Metallica's "Enter Sandman" ripped across the field. The fans were going absolutely crazy, jumping up and down in their seats and screaming. I let myself soak it in for a moment. Then it was go time.

I walked across the warning track, jogged across the grass to the infield, and walked to the pitcher's mound, just like I always did. I was nervous, but I knew all I had to do was get *one* out to end the inning. I prayed. And then I turned my focus on the batter, Wilson Valdez. After a bit of a battle, he hit a bloop single to center that scored a run and advanced another runner to second. Now it was 8-5, and I still had two men on base.

Ben Francisco came to bat, and he hit a double to the left field gap. 8-7. Unbelievable.

I remember praying the whole time I was out there, "Lord, have mercy! Please let this come through." I doubt there was anyone in the stands thinking I was going to get it done. It was funny because it was always the guy I didn't expect, the guys I didn't know, who gave me trouble. For example, Jayson Werth was *supposed* to give me trouble. I was conscious of him. The difficult thing was the guy coming in off the bench who had no expectations on him. They're the guys who will kill you.

We intentionally walked Werth, loading the bases, and Raul Ibanez came up. I hadn't faced him a lot, but I had confidence about getting this done. I felt like God was saying, "Just relax—just do what you do. Don't worry about what everybody is expecting." I got to work, and it worked out. Ibanez struck out swinging to end the eighth. The stadium went nuts and I went to the dugout, struggling to get my emotions under control.

You wouldn't believe the talk I was having inside my head. Every negative thought in the world was coming at me, and I was trying to battle them back. I was praying, asking for help to do what I needed to do. Suddenly a wave of peace like I have never felt washed over me. I knew it could be the last time I was ever on the mound, but I felt okay. I started to enjoy the moment, which was nice for a change; there were so many moments I'd missed because

I was too wound up or too critical of myself.

Despite all the successful games I'd pitched, I knew that final inning was important for me; if we lost, I thought it would brand me as a guy who couldn't pitch in big games. But the peaceful feeling remained. I felt like all 16 years of my career had led to that moment, and I was telling myself, *I'm confident in who I am. I can do this.*

When I went out there for the ninth, I was focused only on what I could control: making good pitches. That was what mattered, not all the fans or that it might be Bobby Cox's last game. The win didn't even matter any more. It was just one pitch at a time. If I threw a good pitch and the guy hit it and we lost the game, I would have done all I could do.

Surrounded by thousands of screaming fans, I was completely at peace. It was about me and the catcher's glove, and what I needed the ball to do in between. The crowd was amazingly loud, but as loud as they were, I could still hear Bobby Cox. He believed in me with all his heart. I took a breath and felt the ball in my left hand. One pitch at a time.

I'd been right about the shadows; they crossed the field between me and home plate, so the batters were at a disadvantage. They could see the fast ball, but they couldn't see the spin of the breaking ball when it crossed from sunshine to shade. Shane Victorino dug into the box, ready to hit. There was nothing left for me to do but pitch. It was completely surreal. I was so relaxed and confident.

Four pitches to Victorino,

Six pitches to Brian Schneider.

Three pitches to Greg Dobbs.

I struck out the side, looking. When I raised my arms up in the air, I felt like a burden had been taken off me. It was my last save, but it felt like my first. My catcher, Brian McCann, came out and hugged me. If the fans had been loud before, now they were absolutely deafening. The crowd was chanting Bobby's name. We formed up and shook hands with the coaches and Bobby like we usually did, and when I got to Bobby I gave him the game ball. He didn't want to keep it, but I made him.

Winning our game was important, but we still had to wait for the outcome of the Giants and Padres game. We went into our clubhouse like we always did, but no one was changing clothes. I knew I would have some explaining to do about my near implosion, and sure enough I was surrounded by reporters wanting to ask what on earth I was doing out there in the eighth inning. I told them, "It was probably a good situation that we had a big enough lead that I couldn't screw it up too bad. Don't think that didn't go through my mind out there, if I screwed this up I'd go home and be a goat." Everything was pretty light-hearted. And given what could have happened, I was glad I could laugh about it. They asked if I was still determined to retire, and I said my decision hadn't changed.

After answering all the questions, the media left the clubhouse and we finally had some time to ourselves. The Giants and Padres were still playing, and I sat at my locker watching the game on the televisions. There was a buildup of emotion as we waited for their game to finish. No matter who won, we were going to play again; we'd taken care of business when we needed to. We had a lot of young guys who had never been in the playoffs before, and now there was a real chance it was going to happen. There were also a couple guys we felt awful for, Martin Prado and Chipper Jones, because they had done so much to help the team get to this point, only to be taken out of the playoffs by injuries.

Soon after the media left, the clubhouse guys started putting up sheets of plastic over the lockers, in case we ended up having a Wild Card celebration involving champagne. Seeing the clubbies putting up the plastic only added to the excitement for the young guys. I watched the faces of the younger players who had never been to the playoffs; as an older player, their excitement made me feel young again.

By the time Brian Wilson, the Giants closer, entered the game, we were all together in the main part of the clubhouse which had been cleared of furniture. Bottles of champagne and cans of beer were sitting on the picnic table or crammed into ice-filled coolers. Some guys were wearing goggles, getting ready for the champagne shower. Thank goodness Brian Wilson made it easy for us! He threw 17 pitches and recorded three quick outs. The Giants beat the Padres, 3-0, and the Braves were the National League Wild Card team. We were going to the playoffs!

It was a great clubhouse celebration. Champagne sprayed everywhere, and guys were opening beers, taking a sip, and dumping the rest down someone's back or over their head. The smell of cigar smoke, champagne, and beer filled the clubhouse. It stunk, but we sure loved it. We were all together, whooping and hollering, which was pretty much how the whole year had been. We were a close-knit group who enjoyed being together. Bobby and the coaches were watching the game in his office, giving us space, and then they came into the clubhouse to join us.

I made sure to shake everyone's hand or give them a hug. I remember talking to Omar Infante because he'd been such an important and surprising part of our success. There weren't any cliques in that clubhouse. We had big name players on our team, but throughout the season, every guy who put on the Braves uniform had helped get us to that point. There wasn't a solitary superstar who carried the team all year long, though McCann was closest to that. There were no 20-game winners among our starting pitchers, but we had guys who were consistent and others who stepped up and played great when we needed them.

We knew that a bunch of fans were still sitting in the stands outside, watching the Giants/Padres game on the big screen. After whooping it up in the clubhouse for about 30 minutes, we raced down the tunnel and out onto the field. It was chilly, especially since most of us were soaked, but we didn't care. There were a couple thousand people still out there, hours after our game had ended. I wasn't surprised because I knew how our team had affected the community. I think they saw us as a bunch of blue collar guys who went to work. We were a gritty, fight-to-the-end kind of team, a reflection of the hardworking people of Atlanta. We came out to say "thank you" to the fans and acknowledge their support as part of our success. At some point, in the midst of all the celebrating, some of the players carried Bobby on their shoulders. It was a fitting tribute.

Finally we were celebrated out. We went back into the clubhouse to clean up, get dressed, and go home. When I got back to the house, I called Sarah and we talked. She and the kids were already in Virginia because school had started. My oldest son Will had played in a tournament that weekend, and Sarah had watched my game on her phone. We reflected on how unbelievable it all was, even after sixteen years in the bigs. I was so grateful that I'd been able to go out there and compete and that God gave me another day.

MY LAST GAME

The last save of my career was like a dream, but the last game of my career wasn't how I expected at all. It's like that line in the movie "Field of Dreams," when the old-timer, Moonlight Graham, is talking about the only game he'd ever played in. He says, "You know, we just don't recognize the most significant moments of our lives while they're happening. Back then I thought, 'Well, there'll be other days." I didn't realize wouldn't be any days after that one.

I knew I was going to retire at the end of 2010, and fully expected to be playing until the end of our run, but that's not how it worked out. My last game came on October 8th in the tenth inning of Game 2 of the National League Division Series between my Atlanta Braves and the San Francisco Giants.

We didn't know it then, but the team we were playing would go on to win the National League Championship Series, downing the

Phillies 4 games to 2, before beating the Texas Rangers in the World Series, 4 games to 1. They were a quality team. They had great starting pitching, some excellent position players—including their rookie catcher, Buster Posey who went on to win the NL Rookie of the Year—and a lights-out closer in Brian Wilson.

The series opened in San Francisco since they won their division. I've never pitched well at AT&T Park. It seems like it's always cold and blustery there. It was always hard for me to get loose, and hard for me to get a good grip on the ball.

Still, our spirits were high, mine included. We were all excited about the possibilities of what we could do. I felt relaxed. On Wednesday, both teams had workouts at AT&T Park. It was also a chance for the media to talk to the managers and the starting pitchers. I just went about my business. Once I finished my workout and got back to the hotel, I didn't leave except to meet up with Takashi Saito and a group of other guys to go out for Japanese food. Everything was low key and I felt prepared.

Game 1 on Thursday night was an outstanding pitching matchup. Derek Lowe started the game for the Braves, while Tim Lincecum pitched for the Giants. Because we lost that first game 1-0, Lowe's pitching performance got overshadowed, but he more than held his own. The Giants only managed five hits and we were able to compete. Unfortunately we only got two hits, and neither came at a key time to score a run.

I warmed up that night, but I never went in. We were far from thinking we were out of the Series. We had only lost the first game, and that was against one of the toughest pitchers in the major leagues. We knew we could hold our own, and we went out determined to prove it in Game 2.

The Game 2 starters were Tommy Hanson for the Braves and Matt Cain for the Giants. They were pretty evenly matched in terms of wins and ERA. We had every confidence in Tommy. He gave up three runs in the first inning and another in the second, but between his four innings and our bullpen, the Giants scored just four runs. Cain and the San Francisco defense were doing their job, too. We left guys on base just about every inning and we didn't get the timely hits we needed. We got one run across in the sixth, but it wasn't until the top of the eighth inning that we got a break. They brought in their closer, Brian Wilson, but we managed to score three runs, tying the game 4-4.

On our side of the field, Bobby had gone to his bullpen early since Hanson left in the fourth inning. There weren't too many arms left. After Hanson, Bobby put in Mike Dunn, Peter Moylan, Jonny Venters, and Craig Kimbrel, who pitched the eighth and ninth innings. I came in to pitch in our half of the tenth inning with the score still tied 4-4.

The Giants pinch hit Edgar Renteria for Mike Fontenot in the 10th. Renteria laid down a perfectly placed bunt toward third. I went to field it and at the last second barely missed running into Troy Glaus, who was charging in from third. I felt a little pinch around my ribcage. I thought it might be cramps, but as I walked back to the mound I could tell something wasn't right. Renteria made it safely to first.

Thinking I'd just gut it out and keep going, I lifted my leg to throw the next pitch. My chest hurt even worse when I delivered the pitch. Andres Torres bunted the ball right back to me, trying to advance Renteria into scoring position at second base. It was a bang-bang play on a routine ball, but as soon as I reached down to scoop it up, I was stunned by a hammer of pain. I couldn't breathe. It felt like I'd been shot in the side. I managed to look over to second but I wasn't going to get Renteria. Somehow I made the play at first.

And then I dropped to my knees in agony.

I didn't know it, but I'd strained my left oblique fielding the Renteria bunt. I've never had pain that could flatten me, but that's where I was: down for the count in the middle of the field during a playoff game. It was as tough a moment as I've ever been in. My team was already playing hurt. The ballgame was tied and my team was counting on me to help them win. The Braves trainer, Jeff Porter, came out and helped me off the field. The feeling that I'd let my team down was a punch to the gut, and knowing it was probably my last game was the haymaker.

We ended up winning the game 5-4, and coming home on the charter flight, the team was upbeat. We'd just had a great comeback win and we felt like things could turn our way in the series if our hitters began to break out back at Turner Field. Everyone was full of hope; everyone but me.

The flight home was agony. I could barely move. Every time I moved, even a little bit, it felt like my chest was going to explode. I couldn't sleep, I couldn't laugh, and I certainly couldn't complain. I didn't want my attitude to bring anyone else down. We'd just won an important game, and even if I never pitched again, if our team kept going in the playoffs or reached the World Series, I would be excited.

I had confidence in our team. We had enough good, healthy pitchers in that bullpen to win the World Series. Besides, we had overcome so much, I figured we could rebound even more. But in terms of my chances of being able to play again, I wasn't optimistic. I could tell that the injury wasn't going to go away with a couple days of rest. Flying back to Atlanta after the game, I had a lot of time to think. I sensed I'd probably thrown my last pitch as a professional. I got to call Sarah, and she was in tears, about as upset as I'd ever heard her. She didn't want me to have any regrets when I retired. She told me how much she hated that I'd been injured, that I'd had a good year and a great career. I reassured her that I wasn't reconsidering my decision. I wouldn't have written my own script to end that way, but I had to deal with the possibility. I wasn't going to play the "what if" game for the rest of my life.

I was 39 years old. Since I couldn't play, and probably couldn't rehab in time, I knew the best thing I could do would be to encourage the young kids. By the time I got back to Atlanta on Saturday morning, I was okay, mentally. My plan was to head to the ballpark the next day, try to suck it up, and play through the injury. And along the way I'd do everything else I could to help the team.

Our plane landed and we took the bus back to Turner Field, and all I had to do was hop in my truck and drive home. I made it into the truck, but I was in so much pain I wasn't sure I was going to be able to drive the whole way. I finally got home around 10:30 in the morning. I hadn't slept at all. Sarah and our four kids had gotten there close to the same time, and they were excited as all get out to see me. Fortunately they didn't jump on me! They've always been good about understanding those things. They just gave me soft hugs and told me how sorry they were that I had gotten hurt.

As lousy as I felt, I knew it was important for me to let them know that sometimes life throws you a curve. Things don't always end the way you want them to. As a father I have to lead by example, so I tried to take my injury in stride, to move forward and make the best of it.

I received a cortisone shot at Turner Field on Saturday, and then another one the next day, before Game 3. Usually you don't get back-to-back cortisone shots, so the doctors and training staff kept asking whether I was *really* going to retire. If I were to go out and pitch with that much cortisone in me, I might be so numb that I would tear something and not even feel it, perhaps compromising the following season. At that point I was willing to do whatever it took to have the possibility of pitching in the postseason, and I knew I wasn't coming back the next year.

The docs told me that even with the two shots I'd be miserable. They were right. Before Game 3 on Sunday, I tried to play catch in the batting cage. I threw a couple pitches and it was all I could do to breathe after I threw the ball. Our bullpen coach, Eddie Perez, was catching me. I asked him to throw it down and away so I'd have to move for it. I missed the ball by more than a foot. That's when I knew I was done. The disappointment hit hard. I'd figured that I probably wouldn't be able to pitch, but the flip side was that I *might* be able to. When I got to the park that day, I hoped there was going to be some miraculous healing and I'd be able to take the mound. It wasn't to be.

We played a closely contested, one-run game that night, but the Giants won 3-2. We were at the edge. We had to win Game 4 to stay alive, and even though I knew I couldn't compete, I wanted that for us, and especially for Bobby.

THE SEASON ENDS

The day of Game 4 was unlike any other day I had experienced in baseball. If we lost, the season would end after that game. Usually when the season was over, the clubbies would pack up all my gear and keep everything until the following season. That day was different because there would be no following season.

I had always wondered how I would feel when the last day of my career finally came. Even now, looking back on it, it's hard to describe. I felt satisfied, *relieved* in a way. I knew I had done everything I could to get to the playoffs when I was healthy, and everything I could to try and overcome this injury. It was hard to go to the stadium knowing I wouldn't be able to pitch and that young kids would be put in situations I would normally be called on to handle. But I felt I was going out on my terms. I had done more than I expected and was content with where I was on the last day of my career. I felt like I was where I was supposed to be.

I got to the ballpark and tried throwing in the cages. The pain made me gasp. I had no velocity or control. It was pretty obvious to everyone that I was done. Still, there was no way I was going to walk away without having tried. There wasn't going to be a doubt in my mind, or in anyone else's, that I might have been able to compete that night. And when it was obvious I couldn't even play catch, let alone pitch, I could live with that. I had peace because I'd given it everything I had.

The trainers, Jeff Porter and Jim Lovell, did everything they could for me: ice, heat, electric stimulation. I wore a rib brace around my middle to give me some support. We were going to do everything we could so that if we made it through the first round, I might be able to play. It was the "walking wounded" in the training room that day. Chipper Jones was rehabbing his knee, and Martin Prado was rehabbing as well. We knew Chipper was unhappy to be where he was. He was playing so well when he got hurt, and he felt like he'd let his teammates down. The wheels on our bus were coming off, and that just meant more pressure on our young players.

Yet even with all the injuries and being down 2 games to 1, the guys were in high spirits. We were sure we were going to win on our home field and take the series back to San Francisco. We had the feeling that maybe, just maybe, we could pull this series out, and we'd be on to Philadelphia.

It was a strange sensation for me that day. There was nothing for me to do to prepare for the game. No warmups, no pitch charts, no scouting reports to read for the tenth time. There was literally no pressure on me to perform, and that's a foreign feeling for a closer! I knew I'd given everything I had, but I knew my team couldn't replace me, and that tore me up. It sounds arrogant to say that, but reputations matter in the playoffs. If Chipper were playing, the Giants pitchers would have had to reckon with him. And I'd earned a certain reputation over the years as well. Other teams knew that "Wags" was going to bring it, and that's the kind of mental edge that can turn a game or a series, to get out there for the final out. I didn't want to end my season or career as a spectator, but that's the hand I was dealt.

As gametime approached, the guys were doing their pre-game prep and all I could do was watch and wish them luck. I wandered around the clubhouse for a while then walked down the tunnel toward the dugout bench. Just like I'd done all season, I stopped to chat with the coaches and Bobby at the bottom of the dugout stairs. He liked to smoke a cigar there before the game, and it was always fun talking to him because I knew I'd learn something new every time.

After the National Anthem, I sat on the bench beside Chipper. We watched the game and talked about the Giants. Every once in a while we'd say something about hunting. Between the fourth and fifth innings, I left the dugout and went to the bullpen for the last time.

I always walked down to the bullpen with Takashi Saito and that night was no exception. We weren't teammates long, but "Sammy" is one of my all-time favorite teammates. We met briefly at the All Star Game in San Francisco in 2007, then reconnected in 2009 when I was picked up by the Boston Red Sox at the end of the season. Since he was a set up guy with Boston and I was a closer, we became friends. We always sat together on the bench because we were the two oldest guys on the team. We spent a lot of time talking about our families and baseball and everything in between.

I remember one time he asked me why I got so nervous even after I'd had so much success. I told him I was only as good as my last game, but he responded that he just took it one pitch at a time. He didn't look ahead any further. That was a key moment for me in learning to enjoy the rest of my final season.

When we got to the bullpen, we sat outside and watched the game. I talked to some of the younger guys like Peter Moylan, Jonny Venters, and Craig Kimbrel. I wanted to give them some insight into what I had seen from the hitters when I was in the dugout. After that, though, all I could do was watch. I was a spectator. We lost another close one that night, 3-2, and that was it. I didn't want to walk across the field, so I started walking back through the tunnel by myself. Beneath the stadium, I could hear the fans cheering and chanting Bobby's name. He'd given so much to the organization;

he was the one who created the successful environment the Braves enjoyed for so long.

I reached the clubhouse just as Bobby came in to talk to the team. The players were standing around him in a circle. Bobby was very emotional, and so was everyone around him. There wasn't a dry eye in the room, and it wasn't because we'd been bounced out of the playoffs—it was because we all cared so much about Bobby, and he'd just managed his final game. I could tell he hadn't rehearsed that moment. It was genuine. He loved this team and he wasn't afraid to show it.

His tears weren't as much because it was his last game; they were more because that team meant so much to him. He'd wanted to win in the playoffs for us. He never wanted the attention for himself. He always took the negatives on his own shoulders and protected his players. All he asked was that they show up and play hard. In baseball, it was assumed that if you got traded or sent away from the Braves during the season, you'd messed up; if you couldn't play for Bobby Cox, you couldn't play anywhere else.

It wasn't until the circle of guys around Bobby broke up that it really hit me; *Hey, I'm in the same boat. This was my last game, too.*

Usually at the end of the season, guys are packing up, walking around, and saying their goodbyes. That night almost everyone was just hanging around. I've never seen that before. It was as if everyone was taking a step back and trying to savor those last few minutes together. We were all relaxed, talking and reminiscing about the season. Even Bobby came back in for a while. I took the opportunity to tell the guys what they meant to me and what it meant to play alongside them that year. We enjoyed each other, not just as ballplayers but as men.

The 2010 Braves were a special group. We wanted each other to succeed. Our attitude came from the idea that when everyone rooted for each other, we'd all go a lot further. We had guys who sacrificed their own stats to make the team better, and we understood that sometimes the little things mean more than the big things.

Finally it was time to go. The Braves had been the team I loved as a kid, and I couldn't have asked God for a better place to end my career. I left everything in my locker for Ben Acree and the clubhouse kids to pack up and send to Virginia. I knew if I went back the next day I'd have to answer questions about retirement and Bobby, and I just didn't want to deal with it. I spoke to Sarah after the game and told her I'd pack up the house and leave early the next morning.

When I got back to the house around midnight, I looked around and thought, *I'm just going to go.* I needed to be with my family. I packed and left two hours later. I drove straight through and picked the kids up from school that afternoon. It was the first day of the rest of my life.

CHAPTER TWO

LEADING OFF

EVERY PROFESSIONAL BALLPLAYER was once a kid, dreaming of the bright lights and fresh-cut grass from the time they could hold a bat or throw a ball. Some kids learned to love baseball on the Little League field or while playing catch with their dad. Some kids had picture perfect lives, with two parents, a comfortable home, food on the table, and a new mitt whenever the old one wore out.

Other kids never had things that easy.

To understand a person, you have to know where they came from. I came from Marion, a small town in southwest Virginia. Like almost everyone else around us, we were poor. Most of the time we had what we needed—and nothing more. Mitts and baseball spikes weren't part of my life.

However, what made my growing-up years difficult wasn't a lack of "stuff." Simply put, my family was dysfunctional. And part of the story I want to tell in this book is that even with all the dysfunction, God was at work in my life. Even as a kid, I was given glimpses of hope—through people and events, even when I was all alone—that showed me things wouldn't always stay the way they were.

When I started writing this book, I talked to my parents and explained that there was no way to tell my life story in a way that made them look perfect. But maybe what happened to me will encourage a kid who's going through a similar situation to hang tough—not to become a pro athlete, necessarily, but just to see what God has for his or her life.

I'm living proof that God can take anyone from anywhere and do good. He can take any circumstance and create something new and better. Just like my life has changed for the better, so have my parents' lives. I believe that's because none of us is ever beyond hope. There's a great verse in the Bible, Jeremiah 29:11, that reads, "'For I know the plans I have for you,' declares the Lord, 'plans to prosper you and not to harm you, plans to give you hope and a future.'"

That's what I had to believe as a dirt-poor kid growing up in rural Virginia: that God had a plan, and it was a good plan, even when I couldn't see it and things were bleak.

LOVE / HATE

My parents started their marriage with several strikes against them. My mom, Yvonne Hall, and my dad, Bill Wagner, married young. When I was born, July 25, 1971, she was 16 and he was 19. Mom was an eighth grade dropout; Dad finished high school. There was never enough money and always too many arguments.

Their two families didn't care for one another, either. Mom's family, the Halls, were transplants to the area. They were a coal-mining family from Pax, West Virginia. My grandpa, Randolph Hall, and my mom would probably have called themselves hillbillies. Grandpa wanted to get out of the coal mines, so around 1954 he moved his family—my grandma Lula Mae and their sons, Randy, Mike, and Cody—to Marion. My grandma was pregnant with my mom at the time. Mom was born near Marion and grew up there. Grandpa worked for the Pepsi Cola bottling plant for years. Granny worked, too, at the Marion Diner. On Fridays she always brought home a treat for me. Grandpa brought me a Friday treat, too: a bottle of "special Dr. Pepper." He said they added extra caramel to the mixture. I loved every sweet sip.

Dad's family, Edward "Buck" Lee and Ruby Wagner, were from Marion and had lived there for generations. The Wagner family was well known for turning out good athletes. Grandpa Wagner played baseball and all of his sons starred on the Marion High School baseball team when they were in high school. There were four boys and they all had nicknames: Hotsey (my Dad), Runt (my uncle Letcher), Brady (my uncle Ben), and Kokie (my uncle Sam). They had a sister named Sally, too. Grandpa Wagner worked at the Southwest Virginia State Hospital (now the Southwest Virginia State Mental Health Facility), which was right there in town. My grandmother worked in sewing or furniture factories. They lived in a part of Marion called the "Brickyard"—on the "other side of the tracks," I suppose you'd have to say.

Dad was in high school when he started dating my mom, who was still in middle school. They got married the day he graduated, June 6, 1970. Dad enlisted in the Army and got shipped to Vietnam three months before I was born. Mom and I went to live with her parents while he was gone. He came home for two weeks of leave soon after I was born, but returned to Vietnam until 1972. Once he got home, Dad left active duty but remained in the Army reserves for 20 years. My parents had a second child, my sister Chasity, who was born in 1973.

My parents had a classic love/hate relationship. Even if their families had liked each other and they'd had enough money, I honestly think neither of my parents was ready to get married or to handle the responsibility of being a parent.

When Mom and Dad divorced in 1976, I was five years old.

THOSE ARE THE BREAKS

When I was four, I was climbing on a jungle gym when I fell and broke my right elbow. I don't remember anything, but I've heard the story too many times. We were living in a little place off Pendleton Street in Marion. Mom took me to the hospital, and my elbow was so bad they had to wait a day for the swelling to go down before it could be set by a specialist in Abingdon.

I was a natural righty then, and I still am. I do everything right handed—eat, hold tools, write, start the lawn mower—everything except pitch.

For six weeks I was in a cast that went from my wrist to just above my elbow. It was one of those heavy plaster casts, and it was summertime, so I'm glad I can't remember the itch or the stink! I was still wearing the cast at my fifth birthday party.

One thing I remember clearly about age four, however, was that I already loved playing baseball. I wasn't about to let a broken elbow keep me from playing with my friends. I just started throwing left-handed, and I kept throwing left-handed for six weeks. When the cast came off, I tried throwing with my right again. The ball barely went anywhere. It was useless. I'd lost a lot of strength in my right arm, while gaining a bunch in my left.

A few years later I was playing football in Grandma Wagner's front yard with my buddy Chip from across the street. He was about the only friend I had. We didn't have a football, but I had a hat, so we'd roll it up, use that.

Grandma's yard wasn't more than 20 yards long and maybe five yards wide. There were flower beds on the side closest to the house and a big ledge with about an 18-foot drop to the road on the other side. If you stepped out of bounds one way, you'd get beat by Grandma, and the other way you'd probably get killed falling to the road. We got real good at staying in bounds.

One afternoon I dove for the hat and Chip landed hard on my right arm, breaking a bone in my forearm. Another trip to the hospital, another cast. By that time, though, I was still throwing left-handed, and even with the cast on I didn't miss out on playing.

Uncle Kokie took me to a K-Mart and bought me a Spalding glove for lefties—he probably didn't spend more than forty bucks on it. I used that mitt through Pony League, high school, and into college. It was a brown outfielder's glove with a blue Spalding logo patch on the wrist strap. I don't remember writing my name on it, because I was pretty much the only kid with a left-handed outfielder's glove. It was definitely worn and used. I never put Neatsfoot oil on it and didn't keep a ball in it, but it still withstood an awful lot. It was the one possession I was really good at keeping track of. I knew I probably wouldn't get another glove.

I had no way of knowing at the time that breaking my right arm would change my life in such a positive way. I think it was God's way of doing something unexplainable so that I would trust Him instead of wondering, *Why is it this way?* It seemed like God was giving me these things, the obstacles and the confrontations and the mental battles and the battles of faith and family, in order to lead me to do something meaningful. I found out later, my podium was going to be baseball.

I was able to have a voice on the baseball field by leading with my faith. Through the ups and downs, my faith was going to be on display. His love for me was going to show. I remember being out on the field sometimes when things were not going well, when I was having a bad game or whatever. I'd get in the self-pity thing—*Why me? Oh no, help me through this!*—and have flashbacks to times when I didn't have anything; when I was going to school and didn't have lunch or the things I needed or wanted.

God was saying to me, "Hey, this is your opportunity. This is your podium from which to do something I need you to do. I've given you financial stability. I've given you a family. I've given you everything you could possibly want, now be this for me. Be my beacon of light. Be there to motivate and inspire, win or lose."

I know it's such a cliché when people win an award and say, "I'd like to thank God for giving me the opportunity…" It might be a cliché, but it's the most heartfelt, truthful thing I could ever say knowing what I went through and what He gave me. There's no way I would be here today to praise Him if it hadn't been for the gifts of love and grace.

When I come across a kid going through tough times, I don't have to hold back. I can say with confidence, "I know where you're coming from, kid, but if it's in the books with God, you can count on it. It's going to be there. He's going to give you all the tools. He wants you to be successful and happy. He'll give you everything you need. It might not be the way you want it to be but He's going to give you everything you need to be an inspiration to someone else. You have to believe, in His name, that it's going to happen."

When I got my 400th save and talked to the media about what it meant to me in terms of my spiritual life, what it meant to know and trust that God was on my side, helping me to have the courage to compete, I know it must have seemed cliché. But it's something that is true and self-evident to me. Every day, God is there helping me, guiding me, and not because I'm successful; because I wasn't always successful.

Being a Christian means taking a burden, taking the criticism, taking just a small piece of the cross He carried, and when you do that—when you take the criticism, when people roll their eyes because you shared a piece of your heart—it's the happiest moment for a Christian. You get to carry a small piece of what Christ carried. You're saying, "This is who I am and what I believe, and I'm proud to say that I'm a Christian. I know I'm not perfect but God is, and I can believe in Him 100%, 24/7, 365 days of the year."

It's amazing to think that God could take something as simple as a broken arm and turn it into a career, but that's what He did. When I began playing baseball seriously, I was a left-handed pitcher and in baseball that makes you even more valuable. The fact that I was known as a hard-throwing, effective, left-handed pitcher only enhanced my value to a team. It was another example of God taking all the bad— the anger, the frustration, the desire for more, even a broken arm—and turning it into something good for me and, more importantly, for His glory.

DAD AND ESTHER

My parents' divorce was an ugly time.

I was coached to tell my mom I didn't love her. That's ugly stuff to say to a kid. I was just trying to survive, and fortunately, I don't have too many vivid memories from those years. I hated that I had no control over my life, and I was already thinking about the day when I could make decisions for myself.

Now that I'm a dad, I can see that my children's lives are so different from my own and the way I was raised. My kids see and feel the love Sarah and I have for them. They know we'll be there for them—good, bad, and anything in between. My parents loved me in their own way, but they were just kids themselves, unprepared for reality.

When our first child, Will, was born, I was 27. I had no idea what I was doing as a parent, and Sarah didn't either. But we knew what we wanted, which was to give our kids the stability and love and opportunity we missed out on. We weren't going to have a child just to say we had one. We wanted there to be a purpose.

When Will was born, I looked at him and smiled. I *knew* that he was going to have a mom and dad his whole life. He was going to have consistent love, even when we moved around. Our marriage relationship would be a priority. We would always find a way to work things out. My children wouldn't have to go through what I had gone through. We were going to be what I wanted so much growing up: a *functional* family.

From the time my parents divorced until I turned 12, I bounced around, living with my mom and then my dad. I think my mom had actual custody, but two years after the split I went to live with my dad when he married Esther Quillen. Unfortunately, she didn't care too much for me, and at the time I didn't care too much for her. We never got along. I wasn't her kid, I wasn't always well behaved, and I wasn't about to listen to what she had to say.

Many years later, stories about me ran in *Sports Illustrated* and the *New York Daily News* that talked about my family. There were some hurt feelings, but the stories also cleared the air. Esther and I have been able to talk and have healthy conversations. She and my dad are divorced, and I rarely see her, but I don't feel any animosity toward her.

Back then, however, she and I had a hate/hate relationship. I didn't make it easy for her, and she and my dad didn't respond well, either. There were times when I came home from school when my dad was at work and Esther was gone. I couldn't get in, so I'd be outside my house, in all kinds of weather, just waiting for someone to come home. Now that I'm a dad, I'd guess they were worried I would get into their things, but that's not what I was thinking at the time. I wanted to be inside when it was cold and wet, and I thought they didn't trust me and didn't want me. I felt rejected.

We disagreed about everything. They liked to eat liver and fish and Brussels sprouts, and I couldn't stand any of it. They would make me sit at the table for hours, until I finished it. I never told Dad this until recently, but there was a gap behind our oven and I figured out how to use my spoon as a catapult. I could flick almost any food straight down that hole.

I wasn't well mannered—I acted out like any other kid who hates the situation he finds himself in. I didn't like that my parents got divorced. I didn't like that my dad gave more attention to his new wife—and their children—than he gave to me. It was confusing and frustrating. In fact, that's one of the main things I remember about my childhood: feeling absolutely frustrated by the lack of control I had over my own life. The only person who didn't seem to have any input into what happened to me was *me*.

LIVING WITH LITTLE

Mom lived in a trailer park with a lot of other poor folks, but at least there was open space between most of the trailers. No one who lived there had anything to boast about and it was pretty grim: lots of dirty, dusty country roads and hillbilly living. I hardly ever wore shoes. Our trailer was a basic single wide, but we had almost ten acres of property. I had a room to myself and so did my mom and my sister. There wasn't much to do indoors, other than watch staticky television and play with our few toys.

Instead, the nearby woods became our playground. I was outside all the time, usually preparing to become the next Bruce Lee or Chuck Norris. Our yard seemed to attract the few kids who lived in the area; they were rough and rowdy so my sister and I had to look out for each other. A couple of the kids I played with the most are in prison now.

I managed to get into trouble from time to time, myself. There was an older kid named Lynn who was considerably bigger than me. I had been taking karate with my uncle and was convinced I was Bruce Lee, even though I was a shrimp. I would take on Lynn, without thinking about my size, and we would try to do serious damage to each other. One time we were fighting in the yard in front of the trailer and Lynn pinned me to the ground. He got his hands around my throat and began choking me. I thought he was going to kill me. Chasity, who was even smaller than me, picked up a baseball bat and whacked Lynn right off me. You'd think common sense would have kicked in then, but no—we started wailing on each other in the dirt. Mom finally came out and pulled him off me.

Sometimes it felt like I spent most of my time in Marion running home after fights. I was the poor kid who didn't back down from anything. If someone talked about my shoes, my pants, my hat that doubled as a football...well, it was on. I had a huge chip on my shoulder. I knew I'd lose seven fights out of ten, but I'd fight anyway. I didn't know it at the time, but that attitude would serve me well decades later when I had to face down some of baseball's best hitters.

I've never taken my kids to see where I grew up, but I've threatened to, especially when they tell me they're bored. They've got a basketball court, plenty of toys and sports equipment, and a nice house full of books and food and video game systems. Kids can say they're bored any time, but I wonder what mine would do if I showed them my old trailer park. What would they think if they had to run barefoot way down the hill to Sandy Bottom just to shoot baskets. I'm sure it would change the way they see their lives—at least until they got bored again!

I have a perspective my kids can never have. They'll never be able to fathom the nasty places I lived in growing up, thank God. That's one of the many blessings of my baseball career. My kids will never have to fight that battle of trying to be accepted or having people turn up their noses at them because of where they live. Sarah and I want to give them clear boundaries and create responsibility. In fact, that's one of the reasons I retired. So many times when I was playing on the road, my children would fly in to see me and I'd end up buying them toys or presents to make the travel easier. Sarah and I told them that when I retired we were going to do things differently. There's a responsible middle ground between having nothing and having too much.

The kids are starting to see that now. Our oldest, Will, understands. He's not materialistic and he's generous with his belongings. They're learning that whether you have a little or a lot, they still need to help out their fellow humans. And they're even reminding me that if we're not generous when we have a little, what makes us think we'll be generous when we have a lot?

I bet if Jesus were walking the earth right now he wouldn't be wearing a fancy suit and driving a $250,000 Bentley. We're trying to teach our kids that we are no better and no worse than anyone else. It's not about baseball, or being famous, just like life wasn't just about being poor when I was growing up in Marion. At the end of the day, we're trying to follow God and do the best we can with what He's given us.

SURVIVAL

In 1979, Mom got remarried to a man named George Wohlford. I was close to nine years old. We moved a good bit as my world ebbed and flowed, from nice, big farmhouses to a little trailer where we didn't have anything. Life seemed to go from one extreme to the other, but I'll tell you one thing that came from it—I never minded moving around the minor leagues during my baseball career. No matter how humble the place I lived was, I'd lived in worse. My upbringing made me very adaptable.

At first things were good between Mom and George, but they soured pretty fast. George was an alcoholic. He was abusive, physically and verbally, to my mom, Chasity, and me. We learned to live with it for a while, but the end of the road came one day in 1983.

Mom, George, Chasity, and I went to a lake with some of George's friends. I was about 12. Mom was deathly afraid of water. If we went to a lake, she would only wade out in the water until it reached her shins. George and his buddies were doing a lot of drinking, and George got really drunk. He and Mom were having a heated argument about something while she stood in the water. He grabbed her and held her head under. I walked out into the water and punched George in the face. I grabbed my mom and Chasity, and then we got in the truck and left.

Mom and George divorced soon after. Mom says I saved her life. I don't know about that—I just did what I had to when someone was hurting her. To this day, I'm very protective of her. The day I punched George, I told Mom I would always take care of her. I told her someday I would have money and would buy her a house and a car. That's what I've done because I love her.

After Mom and George got divorced, my sister and I lived with Mom for a little while in the trailer. We went through some tough times. She was doing what she could to take care of us on her own, but it wasn't easy. We never had enough of anything, and there was no end in sight. Even when we got help, it could turn out to be a bad experience.

I was one of those kids who had to go through the lunch line at school for the free lunch. Nowadays teachers are careful about not pointing out who gets free lunch, but back then it was different. I had to carry a red ticket to get my lunch, and a red ticket meant I'd get teased relentlessly. To make things worse, some teacher would announce, "Here's your free lunch." It was humiliating. Sometimes all we had for breakfast was crackers and water, and supper might be the same, but I would skip eating lunch at school just to avoid that red ticket.

Besides not having enough food at my mom's place, I didn't have the right kind of friends. Now I'd call them the juvenile delinquent crowd. The two I hung around the most are in prison now. One summer I stayed with my dad, and when I came back to the trailer I discovered that my closest friend, Keith, had grown about six inches and put on twenty pounds of muscle. I saw him hanging with an older kid who was always in trouble. When Keith saw me, he pulled out a 12-inch Bowie knife. We stopped hanging out together after that—I honestly thought he might stab someone.

That's how it was: more like trying to survive than growing up.

There was no way Mom was going to get a good paying job with an eighth-grade education. She waitressed at a local restaurant and always worked a second job, as a cashier or in an office. We lived a long way from our school and her jobs. She needed someone to watch Chasity and me when she wasn't there. She knew we needed more stability, and even though it hurt, Chasity and I packed up our things and went to live with our grandparents, the Halls.

GRANDPA AND GRANDMA HALL

Living with my grandparents until I was ready to enter high school gave me the greatest stability I'd had in my life to that point. Grandpa Hall couldn't read or write. He didn't drive, so I couldn't play sports because I had no way to get to practice. That was hard, but I knew I was living with people who cared for me; there was always food on the table and the door was always open. Grandpa Hall let me know he was glad to have me there, and Grandma was a strong Christian woman who took me to church several times a week. They were strict disciplinarians, but it was because they loved us.

I owe so much to my Grandpa and Grandma. We had a simple life, but what they gave me wasn't conditional or temporary. They loved me, trained me, and had a big part in molding me into the man I am today.

My grandparents' house was unique. Grandpa Hall literally built it by himself, so nothing was *quite* plumb. Most of the doorways were crooked, and if you dropped a ball on the floor it would roll toward one of the corners. A humungous wood cook stove sat in the kitchen. Grandma cooked on it and it warmed the house. There were two bedrooms, one for my grandparents and one for Chasity and me, until later when Grandpa added on a bedroom for me. The rooms were dark and cold, but Grandma had plenty of quilts.

We had running water for the sink and bathtub, but for a long time we didn't have an indoor toilet. To get to the outhouse we had to go out the back door, around the barn, up a hill, and there it stood, right by the dog pen. It's not fun to walk out into the dark to use an outhouse, but as a kid I didn't think anything about it. When we finally got indoor plumbing—we got a septic tank, and Grandpa, my uncle, and I dug the pit—I thought it was the greatest thing in the world. It was easy to be grateful after hardly having anything.

Grandma Hall and I watched Braves baseball games and Westerns with Roy Rogers and John Wayne. She would sit up late and watch the games with me, and she always kept score in a book on her lap. Grandpa would sit in his chair and watch with us sometimes, and their company

Grandma Hall used basic spiral notebooks to keep score. She didn't make a grid, she just had a lineup and wrote out what happened: "double play" for instance, or "home run." She'd draw the lines to show a hit, and move the line forward when there was another hit. I don't know how she learned, but I thought it was fascinating that she kept score. It enhanced the way she followed the game. Her handwriting was neat. She loved baseball and even the scorebooks showed that. She was all in.

Grandpa Hall had more common sense than anyone. He couldn't read or teach you which fork to eat a salad with, but he knew how to survive. When I'd get frustrated or mad, he'd give me a pick, a shovel, and a wheelbarrow. Then he'd send me to the hill out in back of the house and tell me to dig until I worked out my frustration. I'd chip away at that hill for hours. I'd have blistered hands, but I wasn't frustrated anymore!

That was their way of dealing with me. Instead of sending me away because they couldn't handle me anymore, they found ways to channel my anger or frustration. They never wanted me to go, no matter how hard things got.

Grandpa and Grandma Hall showed me what God was all about. They read their Bible every day, but it was more than just the Bible reading. It was the way they lived, taking care of me and loving me unconditionally and never quitting. I was negative, and I didn't think I had a chance in life. Over and over my grandparents reminded me that God would make a way for me, even if I couldn't see it yet.

Grandma always told me I was destined to do great things on the ball field. I would look at her like she was crazy when she said that. I counted off all the reasons why that would never happen—no shoes, no equipment, no way to get to practice. Too small, too poor, too far behind. And every time I wondered how I could ever be great, she would remind me that God could do anything.

Just like my mom said I saved her life, I sometimes wonder if Grandpa and Grandma Hall saved mine. I'll tell you, I don't know how I avoided social services or foster care. Once I had to stand in front of a judge who asked me who I wanted to live with. Mom, Dad, and my grandparents were all in the room. What could I say? What *should* I say? I stood there in front of my parents and said I wanted to live with my grandparents. No little kid should have to make a decision like that, but at least I had the option to live with two people who loved me.

As a kid, I never really thought about whether my life was *normal* or not—I was too busy living it to think about it. Besides, I was never in one place long enough to say, "Okay, now *this* is normal." All I knew was that the easiest part of my life was when I was staying with the Halls. I knew what I was getting every day. I knew I wouldn't be able to play sports, but I knew there would be food on the table.

I hardly ever played a full season of baseball or football, what with all the moving and no equipment and no way to get to practice. I spent most of my time learning to play sports in the back yard, throwing the ball against trees or making up my own game. I played against Chasity a lot, too—she was my biggest competitor, and tough as they came.

So if you'd asked me back then what made me happy, I wouldn't have known how to answer. Was "happy" getting to play a game, only to go home to Dad's where I'd be yelled at? Was "happy" watching a Braves game with my grandparents, only to wonder if I'd ever step on the diamond again?

I was happy just surviving the day with a roof over my head and something to eat. I was passed around so many times that I didn't feel like anyone wanted me, and I didn't know what *I* wanted, either. I never felt the freedom to be happy. The simple truth was that I just didn't fit in, with anybody.

GETTIN' SAVED

At Grandpa and Grandma Hall's I spent most of my free time in church. It seemed like we were always praying for something to change, praying for something to go our way. My grandma had faith in God, read the Bible, and believed people could be good and that God was in control. We went to the Freedom Tabernacle Baptist Church where Mike Sage was the preacher. He's *still* the preacher there, and over the years he's had a huge impact on my life.

Pastor Mike could see I was in pain. He knew how frustrated I was, but he didn't try to hand me empty words. He was easygoing and friendly, and he told me the truth. He made me feel special, calling me a little "towhead" and including me in all kinds of activities at the church. If he asked me, I said yes. I even agreed to sing in the choir, and that made me feel important and valuable. Someone finally wanted to include me and valued what I could do.

No matter what happened, Pastor Mike always said there was a purpose for everything that happened in our lives. Some preachers only talk about the good parts of life, or they make it sound like nothing will go wrong if you're living the Christian life.

Even as a kid, I knew *that* wasn't true. Life is filled with ups and downs, no matter who you are. Now, when I was young, there wasn't a whole lot of evidence that God had a purpose for everything that was happening to me. I didn't really feel like God was smiling on me. When I lived with my mom, we had nothing; when I lived with my dad and step-mom, all we did was fight. When I lived with the Halls, they didn't have the means to give me opportunities to play sports. My Wagner grandparents were probably in the best position to provide for me financially, but my Grandpa Buck was difficult to get along with because I was such an active kid.

With all that stacked against me, it became clear to me that I needed something I could believe in. Pastor Mike Sage spoke of how gracious and good God was, even during trials and tribulations. He said we should *expect* trouble in life, but he also told me that God would never give me anything I couldn't handle. It was a reassurance that no matter what happened, even if it got hard and things weren't going the way I wanted, there was a purpose to the madness.

I didn't think all my problems were going to disappear just because I became a Christian, but if there was one thing a kid like me needed, it was somebody to talk to. I needed to be able to say, "What the heck, here? I need some help!" Pastor Mike showed me that "somebody" was actually God, and He was always listening.

Life was tough. It felt like nothing was going to go our way and nothing was going to change. I would lie in bed at night, praying to God, telling Him that we didn't have anything. "We need your help," I'd pray, "and we need you to provide for us."

I was angry at everything, all the time. I couldn't relax. Mom got tired of me punching holes in the wall of the house, so she told me to go outside and hit the tree. I remember punching the tree over and over, taking my frustration and anger out on the rough bark. I knew I needed to find some peace, somehow. I knew I needed to change, and I knew I couldn't change myself.

On July 4th, 1982, a couple weeks before I turned 12, I was baptized in the South Holsten River on a picture-perfect day. People lined the bank and walked down into the water to meet the pastor. We were all so proud and happy. Even though I was only a kid, I felt like I was 25. I knew I had to be responsible because of how unpredictable my life was. I'd been told that Jesus was real and could change my life if I trusted him. Getting baptized was almost like a test I gave myself: did I *really* believe, despite how hard things were?

I did. I said I believed and went under the water and gave my life to Jesus.

Look, I'm not trying to thump anyone over the head with a Bible. You picked up a book with a baseball player on the front, not some preacher. I'm just trying to help you understand where I came from, and who I became, and I'd be lying if I said that becoming a Christian when I was 11 had nothing to do with my career as a relief pitcher. Becoming a Christian didn't change my circumstances.

It changed *me*.

When you're a kid you have to depend on other people. I hated that because I'd been let down so often. But when I became a Christian, I found out I could depend on someone who would never let me down. That gave me hope. It meant I might not be stuck where I was forever. It meant my life might change. And when my life *did* change, I knew it was God taking care of me because He loved me.

I'm not ashamed to stand up and say this is what I believe. I'm also not afraid to stand up and say I'm not perfect. Through all the temptations and backsliding and poor choices, God has been working on me to make me into who He wants me to be. Hardship is part of His plan to show me where He wants me to be. And trust me—in the rest of this book, you're going to wonder how anyone could make as many mistakes as I have and still come out the other side in one piece!

God knows my heart is in the right place and that my ultimate goal is to live for Him, and to give and be as good to others as I can possibly be. Gettin' saved as a kid is where all that started, and to this day it hasn't stopped.

Now, let's get back to baseball. I'm going to tell you about a dairy barn in Tannersville, Uncle Jack and Aunt Sally, and how I took my first small step toward professional baseball.

CHAPTER THREE

MIDDLE INNINGS

MY COUSIN, JEFF LAMIE, was two years older than me. He knew part of me was miserable, not because I was living with my grandparents, but because I wasn't able to play sports. I had a ton of energy and emotion, and football and baseball gave me a place to channel all that. So the summer before I was supposed to enter eighth grade, Jeff took it on himself to speak to his parents, my dad's sister, Sally, and her husband, Jack, about me moving in with their family.

Aunt Sally and Uncle Jack lived in Tannersville, a good 45-minute drive from Marion. They had good jobs and were able to take care of their family, but they certainly weren't wealthy. Uncle Jack worked as a heavy machinery equipment mechanic for a coal mining company. Besides Jeff, they had two daughters, Jackie and Cindy. I always looked up to Jeff. He was naturally smart and a great athlete.

I still don't know why, but Aunt Sally and Uncle Jack liked Jeff's idea. One day they picked me up from my grandparent's house so I could go with their family to the lake. While we were there, they asked me if I would like to live with them, go to high school at Tazewell, and be able to play sports. Even though it was a significant moment for me, I didn't hear a voice from heaven or see the sun breaking through the clouds. At that point in my life I thought, *I've moved around so much, what's one more place? And if it means I can play sports...*

Grandpa Hall put up a fight. He'd seen too many people taking me in and pitching me out and hurting me in the process. It took a bit of convincing before Uncle Jack and Aunt Sally were able to gain his confidence. Before things were settled, I walked into the room and saw Grandpa crying. I'd never seen him cry before. He didn't want to lose me and he couldn't bear to see anything bad happen to me.

Eventually he agreed to let me go. He saw that it would be a good opportunity for me, and he knew I would be safe. Uncle Jack and Aunt Sally didn't have a lot, and they already had three children of their own, but they took me on. They did everything they could to help me. I'm still not sure why, but I sure am grateful.

TANNERSVILLE

I made it a point to go see my grandparents as much as I could. I tried to repay their commitment to me in kind. They didn't have transportation, so they couldn't come see me in Tannersville or watch me play sports, but I'd get rides back to their house with Aunt Sally to visit for a day or sometimes spend the night. I enjoyed it, even though there wasn't much for a high school kid to do. Our relationship wasn't about material stuff; it was about irreplaceable company. They lived a simple, faithful life, and I loved being with them. I knew I was loved for who I was.

I saw my parents even less during my time in Tannersville. Mom was living in Lynchburg, and Dad was still married to Esther. It was an uncomfortable period in our relationship, and other than my trips to see the Halls, I tried to stay close to my new home at the Lamies.

Life was stable with Jack and Sally. When I first moved in I had a fresh mouth and an attitude, but they gave me a chance to settle in, and I did. Jeff was the biggest influence on me. He never said a lot, but his actions set the tone for how I wanted to live.

Tannersville was a small town. The population was about 360 people, and most folks farmed for a living and raised hay, cattle, and tobacco. It had one store that served as post office, grocery, and anything else you might need. It had one stop sign.

The Lamies lived in an old farmhouse way out in the country. Jack had received a bonus just before I moved in, so when I got there we did some work on the house. We put on a new tin roof, a new porch, and generally fixed it up a bit. It was a nice place—way nicer than anywhere I'd lived before. At first I shared a room with Jeff, but when Jackie graduated from high school and moved out, the rest of us kids got our own rooms. We could watch television, as long as we were willing to go outside and rotate the antenna by hand. If we were lucky we could get four channels.

I'd moved to Tannersville to play sports, but I discovered that I really enjoyed the winter. If it snowed, we stayed inside and got out the playing cards and Pictionary. I got hosed when we played penny poker—if I had a good hand I was all giggles and smiles and no one would bid. But it was always fun to be with family who cared about me. It still wasn't my "real" family, but the Lamies gave me what they could. In hindsight, they gave me a lot more than a chance to play ball...they gave me a chance to stabilize and get ready for the next chapter of my life.

FELLOWSHIP

Other than me and my cousins, there weren't many kids in Tannersville. We all rode the bus to school. It was a short green bus that we nicknamed "Sweet Pickles." In the morning I'd get on and go straight to the back, where I'd stretch out and promptly fall asleep. I had one buddy I did things with, Aaron Peery. We played football and baseball together and sometimes we'd wade or go fishing in Little Tumbling Creek. Aaron was more of a country boy than I was. He loved hunting and fishing. I was more about sports.

When I wanted to play catch I usually threw in the cow pasture or against the old dairy barn.

This dairy barn was a special place. I went there to let off steam, and tossing fastballs was a lot healthier than punching a tree and a lot easier than shoveling a hillside. I threw against the barn for hours. The sides were wood, but ringing the bottom was a concrete base that made the perfect strike zone. My little cousin, Cindy, would sit out by the barn and chart my pitches sometimes. Uncle Jack would sit on the porch and watch me throw against that wall for hours.

I didn't have good mechanics at the time, but that was how I learned to pitch. The more I threw against the barn, the stronger my arm got. And when I got sick of smacking the ball against the wall, I'd throw in the cow pasture. I didn't have many baseballs or anyone to play with, so I'd throw each ball as far as I could and then run down the field to retrieve them. Then I'd throw them back, sort of a one-man long toss.

When I wasn't at school or pitching at home, I was usually at the little Baptist church in Tannersville where Jack's brother, Gary, was the pastor. I used to go to the Fellowship of Christian Athletes meetings. In spite of my immaturity, I always felt like God was real in my life. I never forgot what Pastor Mike and Grandma Hall had always told me, that there was a purpose to everything that had happened. I believed God had a plan and was preparing me. But what *was* the plan? As a teenager, I kept feeling like everything was building toward something that was always just out of sight, just out of reach.

HIGH SCHOOL

When I chose to move to Tannersville I had no way of knowing how it would transform my life. It wasn't just having opportunities for a better education and to participate in sports. More importantly, I had rules to live by and expectations to live up to. Uncle Jack and

Aunt Sally required us to earn a C or better if we wanted to play sports, and they enforced it. Freshman year I got a D in Earth Science and had to leave the football team. That was hard, but it gave me a goal. I knew I had to turn in my homework, study, and do well on tests if I wanted to play football and baseball.

The year I moved in with Uncle Jack and Aunt Sally, I was supposed to enter the eighth grade. Since I'd failed a couple of grades and was older, I was promoted from eighth to ninth grade on the first day, and I was *not* equipped to be in high school. I'd attended eleven different schools and my study skills were terrible. Mom had never been able to help me much, and Dad didn't have the patience to help me. Grandma Hall, bless her heart, could write and balance a checkbook, but my schooling was over her head.

I liked going to school. I simply didn't have the academic background I needed to succeed. Schools were different back then, especially in rural southwest Virginia. Tutors weren't available to intervene or get you up to speed. My coaches and teachers didn't know my situation. Although I wasn't tested at the time, I'm certain I had significant learning disabilities—a fact confirmed by watching my son have the same struggles in school before he was diagnosed.

Tests were my nemesis. I'd study and study, only to fail. My aunt and uncle would quiz me and I'd know the material cold. Then I'd take the test and feel good, only to see a red D or F on the top when I got it back. I couldn't seem to get what I knew in my head onto the paper.

Once I had to make a seventy percent or better on a biology test to keep playing baseball. Needless to say, I was highly motivated! I studied and studied, took the test, and ended up with a sixty-five percent. When Mr. Kinzer showed me the test I thought, *You've got to be kidding!* I knew the answers, and somehow I'd still managed to blow it. I went home thinking my baseball season was over.

Jeff knew how hard I'd studied because he'd helped quiz me.

He talked to his parents and convinced them that I knew the material in my head, and fortunately they listened to him and let me play. Oddly enough, about five years ago I was at an alpaca auction and I started chatting with my old biology teacher. We talked about breeding, genetics, and DNA, and suddenly he looked at me and said, "You really *did* know this stuff, didn't you? I wish I had known you had a learning disability at the time!"

I wish he'd known, too. I wish *I'd* known!

Despite my difficulties, and because of Uncle Jack and Aunt Sally's support and expectations, I graduated with a 2.7 grade point average. I worked as hard for those C's as valedictorians do for their A's. My teachers were usually as fair to me as possible without just handing me a grade, which was a big difference from my elementary school years in Marion and the other places I went to school. I'm sure I was a handful for my teachers, but their usual response was to tell me I would never amount to anything.

Academics definitely took a great deal of my attention in high school, since I needed to work so hard to keep up; but those four years were about a whole lot more. I met coaches and other mentors who became lifelong friends and encouragers. I finally had a support system of people who liked me and believed in me *and* made it possible for me to play ball. I became more laid back and relaxed and watched some of my anger drain away. I'd always felt like everyone else was walking ahead of me and I was constantly running to catch up. High school is where I began to learn who I wanted to be and what I wanted to make of my life.

My life to that point had been a fight, but in Tannersville God gave me a breather.

HIGH SCHOOL SPORTS

Playing sports year round changed everything. I'd never finished a full season of baseball or had a consistent coach, and my game was really rough. Growing up I'd never been able to throw very hard and I wasn't very big, so pitching was always a stretch. When I started high school, I was still about 4'11" and 85 pounds soaking wet.

When I did pitch, though, I was effective, even if I wasn't intimidating. In high school I was throwing in the low eighties, which is pretty good for a kid that age. I was too skeptical to realize I was good—I just figured I was getting lucky.

By the time I started playing high school ball I had a very strong arm. I didn't actually *throw* very hard, but my mechanics made up for it. Close your eyes and imagine the worst pitching mechanics you can. Okay, you just pictured me at age 13. I'd been watching the Atlanta Braves my whole life, so I had a big league ideal in my mind. When I pitched, my glove went way over my head, I kicked my leg as high as I could, and who knows what the rest of my body was doing. I was a wildman. I had no clue where each pitch would end up—I just hoped the catcher could catch it! I was pretty successful, but didn't know why. Looking back, it was a combination of hard work and being effectively wild.

My favorite position was centerfield. I loved running and diving for a fly ball. There wasn't anything better than making a diving catch or throwing someone out at home plate. I liked hitting, too, and I loved stealing bases. The theme here is that I loved getting dirty, which might be why I didn't like pitching as much. It was fun to come in after a game with dirt on my uniform; it made me feel like I'd done something.

As much as I enjoyed baseball, I enjoyed football even more. My arm was better conditioned for throwing a football, and I split my time between defensive back, running back, and quarterback. Junior year I was quarterbacking and broke my collarbone during the second game. It was a lost season, but when football started up my senior year I was back taking snaps again.

My nerves were terrible. When I quarterbacked, there were times I had to call a timeout because I'd be throwing up or hyperventilating in the huddle. It was unbelievable. I wasn't good at calling or running plays, but I was able to adapt. I had survival skills. I enjoyed the hitting and running, and I felt like I could always out-compete the other team despite my small size and shaky nerves.

It wasn't much different when I pitched. I'd repeat to myself, "I can't mess this up—what am I gonna do?!" Playing the outfield was no big deal, but pitching gave me a bad case of the shakes...not exactly major league relief material!

The more I pitched, the better I did. People started to have expectations about my performance, but my expectations outdid anything people could put on me. I wanted to win in a dominating fashion. To feel successful I needed to strike out twelve or fifteen guys, go 3 for 3, and steal a couple of bases. I put that pressure on myself, and no coach has ever been as hard on me as I am. To succeed I had to learn how to control my body and my mind. For years I didn't think it was going to happen. I began to pray on the mound to try to calm myself, and it was standing alone with the ball in my hand, facing a batter, that I learned to lean on God for the confidence I needed.

Still, there was no reason to believe I'd be a big leaguer. Even though there were minor league teams around the area, the thought that a small town kid from our neck of the woods could make it to the big leagues seemed like a fantasy. In fact, I never even considered it. Plus, my past had conditioned me not to hope—high expectations only meant greater disappointment.

Most of my family and friends told me I was too little to play. In some ways I look back and thank them for saying that. It motivated me. I wasn't anything special to look at. I wasn't tall. I wasn't strong looking or even that fast. If I had been looking at myself from the outside, I probably would have thought the same things. There was a key difference, though—God gave me belief in myself that no one could take away. My strength was through Him, even when I didn't *know* that it was through Him. Even those times when

I was throwing up or shaking with nerves, I knew I was capable of what I was trying to accomplish.

The friends are what I'll remember most about high school baseball. I pitched a no-hitter as a sophomore, and we went to the state championships for the first time in school history my senior year. I was named the Virginia Player of the Year once and made All-State as both a pitcher and centerfielder. But hanging out at my teammate's homes, joking in the dugout, riding the bus to away games, listening to Coach Peery...those are the memories I'll have forever. I finally felt like I belonged.

TRAJECTORY

The summer between my junior and senior years of high school, I went to a tryout camp for the Bluefield Orioles up in Bluefield, West Virginia. I didn't want to pitch so I tried out in the outfield. We were in Bowen Field, and the centerfield fence read "365 feet." The coaches hit fly balls and ground balls out to us and we threw back to the bases. I wanted to show off my arm. I stood in center-field, throwing balls into the stands behind home plate, or behind third base. Someone noticed my arm, all right, because I ended up making the tryout All Star team. We played another Oriole affiliate All Star team from the area in a game in Glen Burnie, Maryland, at the beginning of my senior year.

That game I played against juniors and seniors in college. It was my first taste of high-level competition. I played right field and had two at bats. I struck out and hit a double the next time. The guys who were pitching looked like they were throwing about a billion miles per hour. I couldn't have been any more overmatched. But it was a good experience because I saw how I needed to get better. I kept thinking, *I do not belong here.* I was 5 feet 6 inches tall and weighed 135 pounds my senior year. I was playing against guys who were in their early 20s.

That All Star game convinced me I could play college baseball, and it sure seemed like fun! Getting into college, however, was far from certain. I didn't have the SAT scores or the GPA. Even if I got into college, I wasn't sure I could afford it.

Remember how I told you that my Grandma Hall always said I would succeed on the baseball field, and that God had plans for me? Well, part of God's plan was putting people like coach Peery in my life. While I was clueless, he spoke to different schools about me, and during my senior year I was offered a full-ride baseball scholarship to Virginia Tech in Blacksburg, Virginia.

COLLEGE ATHLETICS

As much as I would have *loved* to have my education paid for by playing baseball for Virginia Tech, I turned down the scholarship. My SAT score was too low, and I didn't want to keep retaking the test. Even if the university had worked with me to get me accepted, it would have been too big for me. Between my bad study habits and learning disabilities, I would have gone underwater and never come back up.

But I still wanted to play college sports. I chose Ferrum College, a small private school in Ferrum, Virginia. My cousin Jeff was already there, and I wanted to go somewhere with a friendly face. I thought it would be less overwhelming than Virginia Tech, more like a high school setting. Ferrum was a small enough school that it could work with a student like me to help me succeed on *and* off the field.

The tricky part was the cost. Instead of a free ride at Virginia Tech, I'd have to pay $9000 a year. Dad helped a bit, but like a lot of other students, I paid for college with grants and student loans. When I packed my suitcase for college, I had two pairs of pants, a couple shirts, a pair of shoes and "good luck." I took the same glove my Uncle Kokie bought me at K-Mart. I'd used it in Little League and all through high school, and I figured it would do just fine in college. When you don't have the money to replace things, you find a way to keep using them.

My background said I shouldn't amount to anything, but somehow I found myself at college. I was on my own, making my own decisions, and I didn't have any trouble adjusting. I'd never had money, so being a "broke college student" didn't bother me. I got a job at the library to make spending money. If I worked a full two weeks, I made $48.50. I'd take the check to the bank and cash it for a stack of ones—that made it seem like there was more of it! Then I'd get a haircut, wash my clothes, and go out for a beer and a cheesesteak. Sometimes we'd go to a place called Bowen's where we could get RC Cola and all the fifty-cent hot dogs we could handle. We'd go in there and just crush those things. Now *that* was the life.

You can tell I was a pretty straight arrow in college. The lack of money probably contributed, but there wasn't much trouble to get into at Ferrum. It was a small school in a small town. Instead, I focused on sports. Freshman year I played both football and baseball, though I actually went to Ferrum to play football. Baseball was what I did in the spring and summer, but football was what I loved. The baseball coach knew me because of my cousin, but the last time he'd seen me in high school my arm wasn't anything outstanding.

Spring of my freshman year, one of the football coaches, Dave Davis, came to a game to watch me pitch. I had a good outing. After the game, he walked me back to the locker room, put his arm around me, and said, "You know, you could play football at Ferrum for four years and do fine, but you're not going to the NFL and you could get hurt. You have a real future in baseball and that's what you should stick with." Then his voice went down a notch. "If you want to play football, Billy, this is what I'm going to do. I will run you to death because you cannot hit."

That was the day I decided to stop playing football and switch to baseball full time! If Coach Davis hadn't said anything, I might have kept playing football. I was always much more successful in baseball than in football, and because I was usually the littlest guy I was always getting beat up. But I liked the action and I liked playing defense because I could do the hitting instead of being hit.

When Coach Davis talked to me that day, it was one of those moments that proved what Pastor Mike and Grandma Hall had been saying all those years. I might have a plan for myself, but God had an even better one.

CAPE COD LEAGUE

In 1992, my sophomore year, we were playing Shenandoah University in Winchester, Virginia. One of the directors of the Cape Cod Baseball League was there. He'd heard about me, and even though I wasn't pitching, he came by to ask if I wanted to play that summer in Cape Cod. I worried about how far away it was and guessed I'd feel lonely. Plus money was tight. But he promised me a job, and it was a great opportunity to play in one of the most prestigious amateur baseball leagues in the United States.

Aunt Sally and Uncle Jack drove me to Cape Cod. It felt like a week of driving and it rained the whole way up. They dropped me off with my host family, the Thorpes, in Brewster, Massachusetts. All I brought were a couple pairs of shorts and pants, a ratty pair of cleats, a Ferrum baseball cap, and a glove I'd used since high school. That wasn't just all I *had*—it was all I *needed* to complete.

However, I was facing a whole new level of competition. I played for the Brewster Whitecaps. My roommate at the Thorpe's house was Darrell Nicholas, a centerfielder from the University of New Orleans. He was a left-handed hitter and he could flat out fly. Another good thing about Darrell was that he had a car and could drive me everywhere.

The Brewster Whitecaps played at the baseball field belonging to Cape Cod Regional Technical High School in Harwich, Massachusets. The field was behind the school, and the outfield fence was a plastic snow fence. There was nothing special about it, and many of the other teams had nicer facilities. We didn't use their locker rooms, so we got dressed at home before we drove to the game. At least they had covered dugouts! It wasn't really much different from where I played at Ferrum...except Ferrum had a scoreboard and a real fence.

One of the first people I met at the ballpark was Todd Walker. He was a freshman at Louisiana State University. Todd was an All American and Freshman of the Year. After we shook hands he asked, "What position are you?"

When I told him I was a left-handed pitcher, he said, "Oh you're a thumber."

I learned a thumber was a pitcher who threw breaking balls. He thought I wasn't going to be a hard thrower and I'd rely on a lot of off-speed pitches and junk, but when he saw me pitch his ideas changed a bit. Nobody had ever seen a lefty as little as I was throwing that hard.

It seemed like everyone I met came from a big school. There were a couple guys from small colleges and a couple coaches from Division 3 schools, but that was about it. Guys from LSU or Wichita would ask me, "Where do you go?" My answer was guaranteed to draw a blank stare. Ferrum was a place you couldn't find unless you were lost.

Playing in the Cape Cod League was a great experience, but at first it was more than a little overwhelming. The League is full of talent, guys who got taken high in the draft. Scouts were always watching from the stands or behind the fence. You couldn't pick your nose without a scout making a note on his clipboard. I was out of my element and I had no idea what to expect. For some guys, the Cape Cod League was part of their plan to make it to the bigs, but I'd only started focusing on baseball one year earlier. I was almost an accidental participant, but I tried not to let that show.

I was figuring out everything on my own. At Ferrum I knew

some people, I was close to family, and I knew who to call if there was a problem. At the start of that summer in New England I didn't know a soul. It was just me: no money, no car, no one to call, and the same glove I'd been using since forever.

Nothing had prepared me for the level of anxiety I felt. One game in Brewster I got on the mound, went through my warm-ups, stepped off the mound, threw up all over the infield grass, and then started pitching. It was crazy. I just pushed through it. I didn't want the fear of the unknown to scare me into inaction. I wanted to see where this road would take me; to see what was possible. In order to do that, I had to take risks. I didn't like it, but I knew I needed to do it anyway.

That summer it seemed like whenever I was about to be held back, something would happen to move me forward. For example, after struggling to find a job that would pay for my summer expenses and help with my next year of school, I ended up working at a mansion on the outskirts of Orleans, one of the little towns there. I was a yard man. I started work at 7 in the morning, and I'd mow grass, sweep the sidewalks, trim shrubs, and pick weeds until 3. Then I'd head to baseball practice. I made $500 a week, and boy, did I think I was rich! I was wondering if I should just shut down this baseball stuff and work!

Things like that kept cropping up. Even at the time I could definitely see how God was working in my life. Proverbs 3:5-6 says, "Trust in the LORD with all your heart and lean not on your own understanding; in all your ways submit to Him, and He will make your paths straight." I definitely had a long way to go in learning to trust God and rely on Him in *all* my ways, but I was starting to understand that He could make my paths straight.

Once I got settled in, my friendships made things easier. I got to know a lot of the guys on my landscaping crew, and we talked about everything. Most of them went to big schools and grew up in cities, so my stories of life in Marion sounded like life on another planet. My host family, the Thorpes, stopped taking rent and we became friends. Mr. Thorpe owned a plumbing business, and he even let me use one of the work trucks to drive to practice and get around Cape Cod. The Thorpes became like a second family to me. They had a nice little house right on the water. Mr. Thorpe would wait up for me and Darrell to get home from baseball games and we'd have ping pong tournaments. I stayed in touch with them after that summer, and in 1999 they came to see me when I was at the All Star Game in Boston.

BOY OF SUMMER

I turned 21 that summer while I was playing at Cape Cod. My mom and Sarah—a wonderful girl I'd started dating at Ferrum—drove up from Virginia to celebrate my birthday, and I'd made the Cape Cod League All Star team as well. Mom and Sarah stayed with the Thorpes and we all got to know each other. Then the day I turned 21, I earned East MVP of the All Star Game and was named Outstanding Pro Prospect for the league. For one of the first times in my life, it seemed like everything was starting to break my way, and I began to have hope for what might come next.

While I was on Cape Cod, I went to my first major league game in Boston. If you're a baseball fan, it doesn't get much better than that. Driving in Boston was overwhelming—it was literally the first big city I'd spent any time in. Darrell had an uncle in Boston who owned a restaurant. It was Darrell, me, and two other guys on the trip. When we walked into the restaurant—Darrell and three white guys—this big African-American guy came up to us and demanded, "What do you boys want?" My heart rate went right back to normal when Darrell laughed at his uncle. That was some of the best food I've ever had—greens, black eyed peas, and chicken, not the type of food you expect to eat in Boston. Darrell called it "soul food" but I just called it home cooking.

After eating we went to Fenway Park, the oldest ballpark in the big leagues. Going through the tunnel to our seats, the noise of the crowd grew louder and louder. When we walked up the steps to our seats, there was the "Green Monster" staring right at us. We were halfway up behind the first base line. Everything in the park looked bright and fresh to us, from the stark white lines to the perfect dirt to the grass that was green as a dream. Mo Vaughn was playing first, Wade Boggs was at third, and the fans were going crazy.

A foul ball got hit in our direction and the tallest guy on our team was prepared to get it when this little guy jumped up to get it, missed it and got hit in the head. Honestly, it was the funniest thing. I couldn't tell you if Boston won or lost that game. We had such a great time.

I loved being at that game, but truthfully it was a little weird as well. To be at my first big league game while simultaneously thinking *I* could be on the field in a couple years' time...well, I didn't know whether to feel excited or tell myself to shut-up.

The summer of 1992 was significant for me, because at age 21, instead of working at a gas station in Marion, I was playing baseball in front of Major League scouts. I had never been so far from home before, or on my own for so long. It was challenging, but it was one of the most important times of my life. It taught me a lot about how to be a man and make good decisions. I learned about friendship and family. And I was playing the best ball of my life.

When I came back from the Cape, I was one of the top draft prospects, and for the first time in my life I experienced the media hype and attention that would surround me for the rest of my career. Agents were calling and people I didn't even know wanted to talk to me. I was completely unprepared. I had no idea how to handle any of it. In one surreal moment, I was throwing a bullpen session at little old Ferrum, prior to my junior year, and the pen was surrounded by scouts holding radar guns.

So what did I do? Well, the first game of my junior year was the worst game of my career. Our team went to Florida for spring break. We played our first game and I pitched about an inning and a third, during which I walked twelve guys. Twelve! We lost big time. Quite a few scouts were there, and I walked off the mound a total wreck, thinking my pro career was over before it had even started.

That experience turned out to be a very good character builder. After excelling all summer in the Cape Cod League, I was forced to go back to school and rebuild myself. I couldn't rest on what I'd already accomplished. If my goal was the big leagues, earning accolades against other college players wasn't enough. I needed to grow up and make adjustments to my game. My teammates at Ferrum rubbed it in pretty good, too! Since I knew it was going to be a year filled with a lot of distractions, I registered for nineteen hours of credit. If I wasn't playing baseball, I was focused on school; and when I wasn't in class or doing homework, I was on the ball field. One or two starts later, I was able to relax, and everything fell into place.

I didn't do it alone, though. Along the way, I had great support from Sarah, my best friend, Erik Robinson, and my teammates and coaches. I knew enough to know I needed people around me to make me smarter and wiser. God put those people in my life for a purpose, keeping me grounded when all the attention started tempting me to have my head in the clouds. Some of those people, like Sarah, have been with me all the way through my career.

I prayed a lot, too. Grandma Hall instilled in me the need to pray all the time. I talked to God about everything. I made it a real point to thank God, especially when things didn't go well. If something bad happened, I thanked Him for giving me the courage to go out and compete or to try something new and scary. I felt like I could be the "real me" with God, even though that meant I was brash and blunt and some of my prayers might have earned me a stern look from Grandma Hall!

There were always naysayers. Some of them even meant well.

My freshman year, I set the record for strikeouts per nine innings for all the divisions in college baseball. But that summer when I went home, my aunt suggested I should revisit the idea of going into the military. I don't think my aunt was trying to discourage me. She was trying to protect me by encouraging me to seek a more secure and certain job. But even that was a test. Instead of giving up, I decided, "No, I'm going to give this baseball thing a chance and stick with it." God doesn't tempt us, but He does test us. It's like a blacksmith tempering a sword because he has to know whether it will hold up in battle or shatter under pressure. God gives us challenges, and He wants us to rise up to meet them. Whether we succeed or fail, God gets the glory because we put our trust in Him.

At the end of that summer in 1992, I clearly had a lot of growing to do. I was a long way from being the ballplayer or the man I needed to be. But the experiences I had in college and playing in the Cape Cod League formed the foundation for the player I would become. Baseball was definitely drawing me closer to God, and I would need that relationship and strength when I began my pro career in the minor leagues. Before I got to pro baseball, though, God knew enough to bring some key people into my life whose influence helped me on and off the field.

CHAPTER FOUR

GAME CHANGERS

NO ONE GETS ANYWHERE by themselves. We *all* have people who influence and shape our lives, for better or for worse. I'm one of the lucky ones who has a lot of "betters"—folks like Grandpa and Grandma Hall, Pastor Mike Sage, my cousin Jeff Lamie.

The people I'm going to introduce you to in this chapter, however, are in a class of their own. They're on my All Star influencer team. I call them game changers because they transformed the way my life developed. These people changed the way I viewed myself and the world around me, and they still do that today. They gave me perspective, stability, and unconditional love, and knowing I had those things outside the lines gave me confidence to perform inside the lines.

Gentle Giant

Every great player has an even greater coach, and mine was Coach Peery. I played baseball all my life, but it wasn't until I played in high school that I learned to love the game. I owe that gift to Lou Peery. We could all tell Coach loved the game himself, and that was contagious. His passion rubbed off on us. He made every practice and game feel like we were in the bigs. Coach was soft spoken and tall, a gentle giant, and when he spoke, we listened. Although he was more apt to give you a hug, he'd kick you in the butt if you needed it. His physical presence and demeanor demanded respect, but once you really knew him you respected him because of who he was. Coach Peery is the best man I have ever known.

He instilled pride in us. He made sure our field always felt like the big leagues—straight lines, neat grass, smooth dirt, and a perfect mound. We always had quality uniforms, and when we suited up before games we felt like we were getting ready for battle. Coach treated us like young men, with respect and never any baby talk. He came to play, and because of that so did we. Coach Peery was one person who truly thought I could "be somebody" and I never forgot that. There wasn't anything I wouldn't do for him, and all his players felt the same way.

Even as a high schooler, I knew I could model my life after Coach Peery. He made me want to give back and help other people. He made me want to be better. Over the years he took a lot of harsh criticism, but he never let it show in his relationships with his students. His Christian faith was tested because there was still a lot of racism in southwest Virginia. I never saw it as a kid at Tazewell High School. To me, Coach was just *Coach*. It wasn't until years later that I learned there were people who wanted to fire him while I was at Tazewell, despite the fact he was one of the most successful coaches in southwest Virginia.

One time, when I was pretty far into my pro career, I heard they were planning on firing Coach Peery. Over the years the mayor and the school board had done all this stuff for me—given me the key to the city, put up signs that said "Home of Billy Wagner, All Star," and that sort of local-boy thing. I told them that if they fired Coach Perry, I wanted that sign taken down. It wasn't about me, it was about how many kids learned to be ballplayers and upstanding young men from Coach. It was about how he fought to give them a sense of purpose and pride. He means more to the young players at Tazewell than any athlete ever can because he's there with them every day. He's been coaching at Tazewell for over 30 years now, and if I could snap my fingers I'd make sure he was there for thirty more.

If someone made a movie about Coach, there wouldn't be a dry eye in the house. And if he got rich off it, I bet he'd turn around and build a new field for his kids and get right back to coaching.

Coach was the one who gave me confidence. He did it by putting me out there, game after game, and challenging me to get better in tough situations. He was the one calling the colleges and telling them, "You've got to come see this kid, he's really got a chance." Coach was the one doing all the work nobody saw, and he did that for all of us. He didn't expect all of us to become major league players, but when we came to practice he expected us to give 110 percent. It was "yes sir!" and "no sir!" Coach gave everything to us, and we gave it right back. Knowing he'd taken time to scout the other team or that he'd arrived early to make sure the field was perfect motivated us to try even harder.

I don't care what many people think, but Coach Peery's opinion matters to me. In 2008 there was an incident in New York where I was called a racist, publicly, by a member of the media. I was playing for the New York Mets at the time, and after a game we lost I asked the media why they were talking to *me* since I hadn't even pitched. They told me no one else was around. I gestured toward the lockers of some teammates who *had* played but hadn't stayed behind to give interviews. "Shocker," I said, pointing at their empty lockers, and I used some pretty rough language. As it turned out, the lockers belonged to Latin players. Later, the host of a show on ESPN called me a racist and said I should be kicked out of baseball. It became a big story in the New York media for a few days. My manager, Willie Randolph, insisted that I apologize to the team.

It was a terrible time for me because it was never my intention to make a racial comment. It was my blunt way of trying to get my teammates to stand up and be accountable for their actions. They could have been from Mars and I still would have called them out.

Coach Peery was one of the first people I called when the story blew up. I didn't want anything to come between me and Coach. He understood what had happened. The whole time we talked I was in tears because I didn't want him to think I was somebody I wasn't. Throughout my career, Coach called me when things weren't going well. He was like a lighthouse to me. No matter the storms— faith, baseball, personal problems, whatever—Coach was steady. He gave good advice and I had the utmost trust in him because I knew he cared about me and my family.

Ask anyone who's played for Coach Peery and they'll tell you the same thing. He's one of the truest men in the world and he makes it his life goal to give kids a chance to succeed. You can't ask for more than that. All you can do is be grateful. I know I am.

CLOSER THAN A BROTHER

I was a senior in high school the first time I met my future best friend, Erik Robinson. At the time, I was being carried off the football field by two doctors. Erik played football for Graham High School, the conference rival of my school, Tazewell High School. Graham High got national exposure on ESPN because they hadn't lost a game in forever *and* they hadn't even been scored on. The reporters talked to me, since we were playing them next. "Oh, we'll score," I predicted confidently. Erik told me later that prior to their game against us, their coaches showed them the clip of me saying, "Oh, we'll score," over and over again.

It was a tough game for Tazewell. In the 4th quarter, I hyperextended my right knee and was taken off the field. Rather than head to the locker room, I stayed on the sidelines to watch the rest of the game. They took it to us, and when the game ended the scoreboard read Graham 19, Tazewell 0. Once the game ended, the team doctors picked me up and carried me toward the locker room. Erik saw them carrying me away, so he ran over and asked, "Are you going be alright for baseball?" I barely knew the guy from the few times I'd played against him, and there he was asking me about baseball—boy, did that burn me up! I couldn't *wait* for baseball. My knee was killing me, but I told him I would be ready.

When baseball season rolled around, we got a little revenge on the Graham G-Men. Erik was one of their pitchers and I didn't get to face him in the regular season, but we ended up playing each other in the district championship. We were on our home field and losing to the G-Men by a couple runs going into the bottom of the 7th. We got two men on and I was up. Perfect. They made a pitching change, and guess who they brought in to face me? Yep, Erik Robinson. "E-Rob" finished his warm ups as his first baseman yelled that I was an easy out.

I dug in and waited. Erik went into his windup. The first pitch came in right where I wanted it and I pulled it for a homerun. Talk about satisfying! I hit another homerun off of Erik that same game, but he loves to remind me about the time he got a hit off of me batting left-handed to break up a no-hitter I had going.

When I went to the Orioles tryout camp up in Bluefield, Erik came out to watch because he lived in the area. He saw me and asked where I was going to college. I told him that I thought I was going to Ferrum—and he said he was going there, too, and he wanted to know if I'd like to be his roommate. If I wasn't already rooming with my cousin, Jeff, I probably would have taken Erik up on his offer.

When I got to college, Erik was the only person I knew on the football team and we got to be close friends. Freshman year, Jeff used to visit his girlfriend on the weekends, so Erik would come and stay with me or I'd go stay with him and we ended up rooming together my last two years at Ferrum after Jeff graduated.

Now we're more like brothers than friends, but we never argue. In fact, we've never even had a disagreement, which might sound unbelievable to you, given my sometimes hotheaded personality. My wife, Sarah, and his wife, AJ, make fun of us because we're so polite to each other. Sarah kids me, saying, "You're not that polite to me—you talk to him better than you talk to me!"

Erik is smart, easy to talk to, and throughout the years he's been one of my greatest encouragers. He's always been there, patting me on my back and telling me I'm doing well. Erik is never negative, so he has a calming influence on me. Back in college, he helped me focus on what needed attention. When it came down to a choice between partying or studying, he'd say, "You need to study." When things got overwhelming my junior year, with all the draft rumors, he was there to take all the phone calls from people who were trying to get to me. He was a buffer between me and stressful situations I couldn't handle. He made sure I was taken care of; I trusted him, and he's never let me down.

In college Erik excelled in ways I never could. He played both football and baseball, plus he was on the Dean's List, served as a peer educator, psychology tutor, the student representative to the Alumni Board of Directors, and the Student Government President his senior year. He graduated with a degree in psychology and stayed in Virginia to start a career in social work, pouring his life into foster kids, at-risk kids, and dysfunctional families. He was out there in the trenches while I was playing baseball. I have mountains of respect for the man.

Once I started to get established in baseball and made some money, I helped him fulfill his passion by setting up a non-profit foundation called Second Chance Learning Center. (I'll tell you more about Second Chance in the last chapter; all you need to know now is that it's an amazing place that helps at-risk kids every day.) It was my way of saying to him, "You mean this much to me. I want to do whatever I can to help you achieve your dreams." Erik invested in me when we were students, and then it was my turn to invest in him. That's what friends do. It isn't about keeping score...it's about rooting for each other to succeed, and backing that up with how we live our lives.

To this day Erik and I think about each other's well-being before our own. We sacrifice to help each other. Our families are close. I'm the godfather to his two kids, and he's "Uncle Erik" to mine. If something ever happened to me or Sarah, he would raise our kids. Erik is bitter that I retired, because I used to invite him to go on the road with me sometimes, and now he's stuck at home in Virginia!

My relationship with Erik has always been easy and comfortable. He's as polished as I am raw—maybe that's why we complement each other so well. He knows my flaws and understands me. I think God put him in my life for a lot of reasons, like giving me confidence, security, and dependability. I don't know what I did to deserve a friend like Erik, but I thank God every day for him. Proverbs 18:24 says that "there are 'friends' who destroy each other, but a real friend sticks closer than a brother." That's Erik. He's a friend that's closer than a brother, and that's a gift that's truly priceless.

EIGHTEEN YEARS AND COUNTING...

I met Sarah Quesenberry freshmen year in college while we were attending the same high school football game, Franklin County versus Pulaski. I was with my friend, Tony Powell, and he was friends with Sarah. He introduced us at the game and we said hello to each other.

The next time I heard about her was from my best friend Erik. In college he was "Mr. Helps Everybody," and when we lived together there was a constant stream of girls in our room, crying on his shoulder and getting counseling. He never dated any of them, but they were always in our room, which made us look pretty cool. Erik met Sarah one day because he saw her crying on his way to class and sat down to talk to her. So Erik kept me posted on who she was dating and what she was doing.

Since Ferrum was such a small college and town, going to games was a big part of our social life. Sarah played basketball and everyone knew her. I used to go to the girls' games and watch her play. Toward the end of our sophomore year, I knew she wasn't dating anyone, so I decided I wanted to ask her out. Maybe I used up all my courage on the pitcher's mound, but breaking the ice with a girl was always hard. I finally got my nerve up and called her, and to my delight she said yes.

I didn't have a car, but my buddy John Hopkins did. We planned to play in a double-header, then John would to take me and Sarah to meet his girlfriend at Radford College, about 90 minutes away and we'd go out to eat. I had $25; that was it. I was worried to death I wouldn't have the money to pay for our meal and whatever else we did. I was also starving because I hadn't eaten at all due to the double-header.

We went to Cracker Barrel for dinner. I ordered my meal: roast beef, green beans, and macaroni and cheese, and I asked Sarah what she wanted. Well, she didn't know how much money I had to spend and she didn't want me to be on the spot, so she asked me to order for her. That's how considerate she is, but at the time it threw me for a loop. It was the first time anyone had asked me to order for them. I didn't want to seem cheap, either, so I ended up ordering her the same I had. Sarah probably ate about three bites in the time it took me to clear my plate—I was just shoveling it down like a hungry wolf. At some point she slid her plate over and asked if I wanted hers. I did.

I know...I don't know why she married me either.

After dinner we went back to John's girlfriend's apartment and watched the movie *Backdraft*. I'm not kidding: I don't think Sarah and I said five words the whole night. I was nervous the whole time, and to make matters worse she sat in the front seat with John while I sat in the back. I imagine she was probably thinking, "He doesn't talk, he wolfs down his food, and he doesn't have a car...not much up-side here." On the other hand, she probably wasn't looking at me thinking I'd make millions of dollars in a few years, so if she was interested, it wasn't for anything I had to offer materially.

I was first attracted to Sarah's athleticism, but I quickly realized how smart and pretty she was. She also had a good head on her shoulders. And unlike me, she had a plan for her life. From the outside she was the complete package. What it took me even longer to learn, mostly because she was so quiet, was that she was an amazing person inside and out. I mean, Sarah has got it goin' *on*. Luckily for me, she was a well-kept secret. She's shy, and her whole family is quiet. When we were dating, they didn't start peppering me with embarrassing stories about Sarah. So I got to know her slowly, and bit by bit I discovered that I couldn't imagine life without her.

The first time I went to meet her father and brothers, they were playing basketball outside. I hadn't played basketball since I was a kid, and I didn't have a clue what I was doing. We were out there playing and they kept telling me to "post up." I thought, "What does that even mean?" Her dad was running me into fences, trying to show me who was boss, but I was too stupid to understand even that. After the game, Sarah went off to get ready to go out while I sat in the living room with her dad. There was a couch, a chair, and a television; Sarah's dad sat down and switched on an NBA game. Then he turned to look at me.

"Do you like pro basketball?"

"No," I answered.

And that was it—crickets for the rest of the time I was waiting! Despite our differences, however, we began dating more and more. She didn't have a clue about baseball, and before we dated she didn't even know I played on the school team. It was only a few months after our first date that I left to play in the Cape Cod League. When she and my mom drove up to see me play in the All Star game, that was the first time she got an inkling of the potential I had in baseball. Thank God she liked me before that for who I was and not for who I might become. Later that year she was there for me when things began to get crazy.

We did have a couple breakups. The first came during our junior year, but fortunately it didn't last long. The second breakup was more serious. It happened when I moved away to Instructional League—a story I'll tell in more detail in a few chapters. Suffice it to say it was a confusing time for me and I wasn't mature enough to maintain a relationship while simultaneously learning what was expected of me in professional baseball. When I finally made it through Instructional League, I knew beyond a doubt that I loved Sarah and needed her with me.

She agreed, and our wedding was one of the best days of my life.

God sure knew what He was doing when He put Sarah in my life. From helping me with essays in college to parenting our kids when I was out on the road pitching, Sarah has been the perfect teammate for the last eighteen years. I honestly don't know where I would be without her.

Other than my grandparents, my family didn't have much of a marriage pedigree. There were a lot more bad examples than there were good ones. When I was thinking about starting a life with Sarah, though, something else worried me: making plans without any stability. I knew what it was like to do without the basics, and even though I was fine living like that, I didn't want that to be our life. I didn't know what would become of my career. I didn't want to jump into something as important as marriage without having something to fall back on financially if baseball didn't work out. Even then I knew that having lots of money wasn't a silver bullet, but hailing from a single-wide in Marion, I also knew that having money would at least mean I could focus on other things that were more important.

I've been asked before what keeps me and Sarah together. Sadly, a marriage that's approaching two decades is becoming more of a rarity these days. The answer I always give is that she's incredibly forgiving!. The first decade of our life together wasn't bliss, despite the money. All my travel and the concerns about life on the road have made things difficult. But Sarah's understanding and love for me and our family makes her stronger—and that makes me stronger. She's not afraid to speak her mind or call me out when I'm not behaving the way I should.

Coming from a dysfunctional family—and that's putting it nicely—I knew I wanted a different outcome. Sarah and I have had our arguments, but we've learned how to compromise. She understood the importance of that much earlier than I did, but that's an area where she's helped me grow and mature as a husband, a father, and a Christian. Sarah keeps me grounded. She reminds me about what's important and what isn't. She was level headed enough for the both of us, and she got us through baseball in one piece.

And the best thing she ever told me? "This is all temporary, Billy. At the end of the day it's going to be more important for you to be called 'Dad' than to be called a baseball player."

Amen, honey. And thank you. I'll love you forever.

CHAPTER FIVE

CALLED UP

THINKING ABOUT MY MENTORS who guided me can make my life seem pretty neat and tidy, but as I was living it the experience was almost the exact opposite. Nothing exemplifies just how far in over my head I was better than the day I signed my first pro contract.

When I was drafted by the Astros, their first offer was $465,000. To a kid who grew up dirt-poor in Marion, that seemed like a ton of money. And when the offer came, Uncle Jack and I were sitting in an old farmhouse without power. With country bumpkins like us, you'd think we'd say, "Sure!"

Uncle Jack was cool, though. He said, "We appreciate your offer. We'll consider it and get back to you."

Gulp.

The baseball draft usually takes place in early June. On draft day, family and friends joined me at my Uncle Jack and Aunt Sally's house. Sarah, my dad and mom, and Jack Toffey, the guy I'd met in Cape Cod who was acting as my agent, were all there. The day was a blur of excitement and nerves. There were television crews at the house; it was a big to-do in a small town like Tannersville. To complicate things, we had no idea who would pick me or where I would go.

This was in the days before the draft was shown all day on

ESPN. This was even before the Internet! We had no idea what was going on. The draft started around 1 o'clock, and because I turned out to be the 12th pick, we didn't have to wait much more than an hour. I thought I was headed to the Boston Red Sox because they'd shown so much interest and talked with my coach. I also knew they had a pick before Houston, so when I answered the phone and heard a voice say, "Hey, this is Brian Granger with the Houston Astros—we just drafted you," my first response was, "Really? Okay."

I know—classy.

Brian Granger was the Astros scout who had watched me, but the contract negotiation was done with Tom Moody and Bill Buckner. Tom and Bill came to Tannersville soon after the draft to work out the details. They had a tough time finding me, literally.

You need to know where you're going when you head to Tannersville since it's all back roads, most of which don't have names. There was one post office, and everybody's address was a "star route." There were no box numbers. I never mailed or received a letter that had a number on it. The post office knew everybody, of course, but I couldn't exactly say to the Houston scout something like, "You go past a place that looks like an old run down ball field and you take a left until you go over the bridge and you come up the hill…" We decided we'd meet them at their hotel and lead them back to our house.

The day they were coming we had a terrible storm. Trees were down, the wind was still howling, and there was water and mud everywhere. By the time we finally met up with them and brought them up to the house, the power had gone out. My aunt had set a Coleman lantern in the middle of the kitchen table, and that's where we sat and negotiated the deal. Tom came into our house wearing saddle shoes, his cardigan tied around his neck, and his hair slicked back like Pat Riley. That's just how he is—but I bet he wondered if he'd wandered onto a redneck movie set.

So when their first offer was $465,000, I know my eyes were

popping. That was more than my uncle, my daddy, or anyone in my family had ever made. It was mind blowing to think we were going to haggle over more, considering where we came from. But that's how the process goes. Heck, if they had come in at $125,000 I would have thought that was good. We didn't have the Internet, so we couldn't look up what players in front of me were getting. I ended up being one of the lowest signed guys in the first round. It was a good draft. I was in the same draft class as Trot Nixon and Alex Rodriguez. We settled on $585,000, which included $15,000 for college.

I was *totally* happy. When you don't have anything to begin with, you don't complain when you finally get something.

THE MINORS: 1993

My first assignment was in Auburn, New York, where I played for the Auburn Astros in the New York/Penn League. This was short season A-ball, the first stop on the way to the bigs. My first paycheck was $191.00 for two weeks. I wouldn't get any signing bonus money until later, so I had to make that last.

Manny Acta was my first manager, and it was his first professional managing job, though he'd go on to manage the Washington Nationals and Cleveland Indians. I had three other roommates my first year, and the four of us lived in a two-bedroom apartment; Nate slept on the couch, Kendall had his own room, and I shared a room with Smitty. We were all pretty full of ourselves. We'd all just gotten out of college, and all of us were good. But we weren't *that* good—not yet.

I didn't know anything about pitching. To me, it was basically throw-as-hard-as-you-can. I didn't even have a pick-off move. The Astros gave me a pitching coach who was an ex-football player, Tad Slowik. He'd played a little baseball, but he also played football in 1984 for Green Bay with one of my high school coaches. Tad's idea of pitching was to go as hard as you could go. "Throw it harder" went right with my personality.

In hindsight, it's funny that the Astros, who, along with other teams, described me as "very raw," didn't send me to a place that had a true pitching coach. Some of what I learned that first year was just how to operate in the world of professional baseball. But I still had a long way to go if I was going to live up to how good I *thought* I was!

Sometimes working with Tad could be comical. Tad didn't have a clear idea of how to teach pitching. I had only been in Auburn a couple days or so and I threw back to back-to-back bullpens. It had been over a month since our college season ended, and I hadn't thrown since. I ended up straining my shoulder, and it was a month before I threw again.

The first game I got in was against the Batavia Red Sox. One of my college teammates, Randy Lawrence, was playing for Batavia. I was starting the game and my pitch limit was 26. I think I gave up one hit, but I only lasted one-third of an inning and I committed four errors. It was awful. There I was, supposedly the top prospect, and I only lasted one out. I wasn't overmatched with my stuff. I was overmatched in my perception of what it would be like to pitch to professional hitters, and that made me inconsistent. My own worst enemy was myself.

I finished the season with a 1-3 record and a 4.08 ERA. I had 31 strikeouts but 25 walks. After the season ended, I was sent to Instructional League in Florida with guys doing rehab and some of the Triple A players. It was a learning curve steep enough to trip a high jumper.

It wasn't the quality of the players that made the difference between college and professional ball. It was more the attitude. In the pros it was every man for himself.

THE MINORS: 1994

The next year I moved on to Quad City, Iowa, playing for the Quad City River Bandits in the Midwest League. We were supposed to be a prospect team, but in reality we stunk.

In the first half of the 1994 season, I went 1-4 with a 4.01 ERA and about 100 strikeouts and 60 walks. I was good and bad at the same time. I would strike out twelve, but walk six or seven. That season I learned how unfair baseball could be when I made the All Star team, but my best friend Mike Grzanich, who was 7-2 with a 2.70 ERA, didn't even get a sniff.

When I got back from the All Star Game, one of the coaches from instructional league, Tom Wiedenbauer, met me at the ballpark. He said, "C'mon, let's walk around." Tom was a quiet guy; I could tell he had authority. We walked over the field and sat on the tarp. He said, "You know, I don't want you to change, but I want your walks to come down. I don't want you to do something you're not ready for, but I want you to make a conscious effort to compete in a different way."

I was used to striking out everybody in college, but Tom talked to me about relaxing and allowing my talent to throw strikes. He gave me a sense of confidence that I was progressing, but he also stressed the need to relax and trust myself and my ability. After all, I was walking guys I had no business walking. That made me think even more about walking guys, and I thought about it so much that I became a mental midget in that department.

The conversation with Tom really freed me up. The second half of my season became the second chapter in a tale of two Billys. I finished the season 8-9 with a 3.29 ERA, with 204 strikeouts and only 91 walks. Now, 91 walks is still a lot, but it would have been well over 100 if I hadn't had that talk with Tom!

After that things started clicking. I've learned since that when you get into pro ball, sometimes you try to be someone you're not, on and off the field. You try to get larger than life, or maybe you're so insecure you go into a shell. And on the field you sometimes try to be a player you're not meant to be. Tom helped me be the pitcher I needed to be on the field, and off the field I got engaged to Sarah. When she finished college in late May, she came to Iowa and stayed with me. Having the love of my life and my best friend near me made a big difference in my outlook and confidence.

Gary Lucas was our pitching coach, but he was much more than that. He was a friend, and he was the first person who really taught me to *love* the game of professional baseball. We worked together on pitching mechanics, but he also let me find out who I was as a pitcher. We talked about how I wanted to compete and who I was when I was competing. I wasn't a polished pitcher, but I was a strong competitor. I wasn't content with that, however. Gary helped me see that I could compete even more effectively if I discovered who I was as a pitcher, and he helped me battle myself and find out my identity.

That's when things got fun. It seemed like we took six- or eight-hour bus trips everywhere. We usually had a double-decker bus, and the players would sit up top while the coaches claimed the bottom. Gary would come up where I was sitting with my pitching buddies, Mike Grzanich and Scott Elarton. We'd dip Copenhagen while Gary told us stories about when he played for the Pirates and Expos. The miles flew by.

That summer I started realizing what it was all about. The season wasn't a total success as far as numbers, but I began understanding the baseball life for the first time...and without that understanding of what the game was really about I knew I'd never succeed.

BASEBALL AND TRAGEDY: 1995

Sarah and I got married in December, 1994, during the off season. The following year we moved on to the Double-A Jackson Generals in Jackson, Mississippi. When you get to Double-A, you're close. In fact you're more likely to get picked up out of Double-A than Triple-A. My manager was Tim Tolman and my pitching coach was Charlie Taylor. I was throwing the ball well and everything seemed to be working out.

It was May 15. We were on a road trip that took us from Jackson to San Antonio, Texas, and then up to Wichita, Kansas. I pitched in Wichita and got a win. When I got back to the hotel, I got a phone call from my manager telling me I'd been placed on the Houston Astros 40-man roster. That was a good sign. If I continued doing what I was doing, sometime that year I'd go to the big leagues, maybe a September call up. I called Sarah back at our apartment in Jackson right away to let her know. She asked if she could tell her dad, and as soon as we got off the phone she called and told him. Excitement was buzzing around the family.

The phone rang around 2 a.m. the next night. Sarah was frantic. I could barely understand what she was telling me, and when I finally understood her, I couldn't believe it. Sarah's father, Steve Quesenberry, and her step-mother, Tina, had been murdered, shot by Dennis Stoneman, the estranged husband of Tina's sister, Teresa.

Teresa had taken a restraining order out on Stoneman because of domestic abuse and was living in hiding, trying to start a new life. She lived near Steve and Tina and they would check on her occasionally to make sure she was doing okay. They heard that Stoneman was looking for Teresa, so they went to check on her. They were parked in front of Teresa's apartment when Stoneman drove up in a truck, jumped out with his .38 caliber handgun, and shot both Steve and Tina in the head. Steve died immediately. Tina died before she reached a hospital. Worst of all, Ross Payne, Tina's 5-year-old son from a previous marriage, was in the back seat of the car and saw everything.

I couldn't stop shaking. My mind was racing as I prayed that what she'd told me wasn't true, somehow. I was overwhelmed with not being there at home with her, and struggling to control myself and figure out my next step. I asked God to give me the strength to help Sarah. I was praying for her and asking God what I should do. Finally, I called my pitching coach and manager to let them know I was leaving. They came to my hotel room to help me get a flight to Mississippi. My roommate, Mike Grzanich, gave me all the money he had. I got a taxi to the airport and flew from Wichita to Dallas and then from Dallas to Jackson. The team owner, Con Maloney, picked me up and took me to my apartment. I was finally with Sarah again.

She was as distraught and wiped out as I'd imagined. We quickly packed the truck and drove all the way to Sarah's mom's house in Pulaski, Virginia. The whole way I thought, *What can I possibly do for her?* I was praying the whole time, asking God to give me wisdom or some words that would comfort her. At that point, I knew there was nothing I could say that would take away her pain. The tragedy was too sudden and too severe. All I could do was be there with her, and wait and pray.

Once we got to Sarah's mom's house, shock took over. Sarah and everyone else there seemed to be walking around like zombies. It was surreal. Her oldest brother, Mark, had already moved out and had his own place, and her youngest brother, Brian, was still in high school, living with his mom. There was a lot going on for those three kids. Their world had changed completely and they didn't know what to do or how to handle it.

It's difficult to put in words how important our faith was. We were both young enough and naive enough to think tragedies like this happened to other people, not us. We were completely unprepared...and then God stepped into our lives and got to work. Through the pain and questions, Sarah became stronger in her faith. She came to understand that her choice was how to respond: would she become angry, or would she love more? Honestly—and it's hard to say this, but I swear it's true—that tragedy changed Sarah and her brothers for the good. Their lives were never the same, and the pain was intense, but they came out the other side transformed.

I was transformed, too. I called the Astros and told them I'd be back when my family was taken care of, which didn't make them too happy. But at that point I didn't really care about baseball. I stayed in Virginia and helped when I could. The only time I remember Sarah and her brothers really breaking down was during the funeral. The Quesenberrys keep their emotions close to the vest. Until you get to know them, you don't know how they feel about anything. They're very reserved and quiet, and to see their emotions on display like that was wrenching.

After more than a week, I flew back to Tulsa to meet up with my team. I had to make a start even though I hadn't picked up a ball since I left. There was no way my stuff could have been any worse that night—I couldn't hit water if I fell out of boat. My mind was still with Sarah and her family, and baseball just didn't seem important enough to claim any of my attention.

The ordeal changed us both. Before Sarah's father was killed, she was laid back, but afterward she became fearful that the same thing could happen again. As a wife, mother, and sister, she became protective, and she guarded her family. Real life had crept into our innocent world and we had to learn to deal with our insecurities and our fears of losing someone we loved. We prayed a lot, cried some, and talked into the wee hours. Baseball was no longer the only thing we cared about, the only thing that mattered, and that was something we'd continue to deal with as our family grew.

BACK TO BASEBALL

In the weeks and months that followed, things clicked back into place in terms of pitching—perhaps because I'd been forced to get some much-needed perspective. Sarah was able to be there, and we talked constantly—about life and baseball and everything in between. I was 2-2 with a 2-something ERA, made the All Star team, and ended up getting called up to the Tucson Toros (Triple A) in the Pacific Coast League. I flew to Tucson while Sarah and my mom packed our stuff and drove from Jackson.

The night I got to Tucson, we were playing Salt Lake City. I got to watch Donne Wall pitch, who everyone considered the mayor of Tucson because he'd been there so long and had done so well. I was supposed to pitch the next day, so I was doing the radar gun, books, and charts. I didn't know anyone on the team, but I could tell this was going to be a whole new experience. A lot of the guys had already been in the big leagues or were just about to get called up.

I made my first start the next night, but I didn't know anything...no signs, no scouting reports, no dugout traditions. It was just me throwing as hard as I could and trying to compete. As I stood there under the bright lights, it hit me how close I was to the big leagues. I needed to do well—and I did! I felt confident and threw the ball the way I wanted. In my first outing that night, I pitched 8 2/3 innings, gave up 3 or 4 runs, and stepped off the mound feeling pretty good about myself. I was going to succeed.

My good feeling didn't last long. Craig McMurtry, Donne Wall, and Jerry Goff came to me after the game. "You pitched well, but that's *not* going to work."

I tried not to let my disappointment show, but I could hardly believe what I'd just heard. It was only my first game—what more did they want from me? Still, what could I say? They'd all had success in Triple A and in the big leagues. I knew I needed to listen to them if I was going to succeed, so I tried to swallow my pride, keep my ears open, and compete even harder.

From then on the other pitchers in Tucson were really hard on me. When I pitched, they would tell me I'd gotten away with poor stuff, that I'd been lucky, that I hadn't thrown enough strikes, that I'd missed my targets. They weren't trying to say I didn't deserve to be there—they were just telling me in no uncertain terms what I needed to work on.

The most important thing they taught me was that I wasn't going to be able to only throw fastballs. If I didn't develop more breaking ball pitches, I was dead meat. Professional hitters had the experience and bat-speed to make mincemeat out of a pure fastball pitcher over time, and the off-speed and breaking pitches would keep those hitters off balance and allow me to set them up for my fastball.

I felt like I was back in college taking a ton of units. My spot in the rotation fell after Donne, and we were like night and day. He could hit a gnat's butt from 500 yards, and I was lucky to hit the side of a barn from ten steps away. He had control, and I was a wildman. And even as I worked on my mechanics so I could be more accurate and throw different pitches, I realized my mind wasn't where it needed to be, either. I didn't really *know* the game, not like the other guys did. They told me what to watch for during games while I was charting pitches, and their insights and predictions blew me away. They were always a few steps ahead of me, mentally and mechanically, and I was running to catch up.

My curveball was like a stray pitbull: nasty, but totally out of control. I could throw one that would drop neat as you please beneath the hitter's bat, and then the next one might roll all the way to the backstop. Jerry Goff was my curveball guru, helping me identify and correct my problem. He showed me that one reason I had trouble with my breaking pitch was my arm angle. I threw the ball as if I was shooting a bow and arrow, my arm coming right past my ear. I wasn't long and balanced like I needed to be.

I had my work cut out for me if I was going to make the leap to the next level. I was overpowering, but I didn't have a good sense for how to approach each batter, much less how to handle even a small skirmish in my battle with each individual batter. My thought was to aim for the middle and throw the ball as hard as I could, but my time at Tucson taught me there was so much more to it than that. Pitching fundamentals and I had always been like oil and water. There weren't a lot of guys like me in baseball, short fireballers with a lot of power. Most lefties were "bob and weave" pitchers with a variety of pitches and lots of off-speed stuff. Craig drilled me on the importance of working on my craft. Working hard was one thing, but I needed to work smart. I needed to be efficient and ef- fective, because the better the competition got, the worse I'd do armed only with a fastball and an attitude.

I took the lessons to heart. I did well that year. I think I was 5- 3, with a 3.18 ERA at Tucson. Craig McMurtry helped me a ton that year, even though he warned me to stay away from him because he didn't want me "tainted" by association. Major League Baseball players went on strike in August 1994, and the strike didn't end until April 2, 1995. Craig was an older player; he had a family he needed to support and he knew he'd probably never get back up to majors, so he became a replacement player during the strike. There were hard feelings toward the replacement players, and a lot of guys didn't want anything to do with them. Craig was one of my closest friends, but when I'd sit with him in the bullpen he'd say, "Don't sit with me. If you sit with me no one will talk to you." I understood why he'd crossed the strike line, and I didn't blame him. Craig helped get me ready to pitch in the major leagues, and I'll always be grateful for that.

I got called up to Houston that September. Because I'd been put on the 40-man roster earlier in the season, getting called up was- n't a huge surprise—but it was still amazing! I was in the dugout during a game in Tucson. My manager, Rick Sweet, called me over and told me I'd been called up, but I wasn't going up until later in the month because the Toros had made the playoffs. I left for the major league team about five days after the playoffs and joined the Astros in New York for a game against the Mets.

I didn't know a soul on the Astros team but it didn't bother me—especially once I met Doug Drabek. The first night I got there, Doug called my room and said, "Listen, 'rook,' be in the lobby tomorrow at 11 o'clock. I'm going to take you to lunch and talk to you."

You better believe I was down there at 10:30, and naturally I waited an hour for Doug to show up. We were joined by Darryl Kile, another pitcher, and catcher Rick Wilkins. We walked over to T.G.I. Fridays, where we got a booth, and they proceeded to school me on how to be a major league ballplayer. It was a crash course! One of the things they told me was that if I went out to lunch or dinner with the established ballplayers, I shouldn't reach for the check. At times those guys would load up the check to prank the rookies, and if I grabbed the check I might find myself with a $5000 tab! At that time it was standard to tip the clubhouse guy $35 a day. At first I thought I only had to pay the one clubbie, but I quickly realized that on getaway day about ten extra people showed up. It got pretty pricey according to Doug and my other instructors, especially because the more money I made, the more I'd be expected to pay per day.

If Tucson was where I earned my degree in how to pitch, Houston was where I earned my degree in how to act as a big leaguer. Everything was new to me, and I was grateful to the guys who showed me the ropes. I had to transition to managing major league money, too. I was handed a stack of money and my first thought was, *Whoo, I'm rich!* I suggested to my roommate that we celebrate by ordering burgers and a six pack of beer from room service. Do you know how much that daggone six pack was? Fifty bucks! I quickly learned to pick up a snack at the clubhouse and ignore the room service menu!

There were no expectations when I got there in September for the Mets game. The team was checking me out at the end of the season, and I was just taking it all in. I was laid back and happy to be in New York, although the adventure soured since I was by myself. Sarah was back in Tucson, packing up our things and moving us to Houston. I called my family but they weren't able to come up for the game, and even if they had cable TV they wouldn't have been able to watch it. Still, it was my first time in the Major Leagues. I was in awe of the whole experience: being in New York City, staying at the Grand Hyatt in Manhattan, suiting up in my Astros uni, and pitching at Shea Stadium. For a kid from a single-wide in Marion, it was something else!

I made my major league debut on September 13, brought in to pitch to Rico Brogna in the 7th inning. The Mets were winning 7-3. I remember the exact moment I got the phone call in the bullpen. You know how you try to act cool in a high-pressure situation, like you have everything under control? That was *not* me. I felt like I was going to puke and I was breathing like I'd just run a marathon. I knew zero about Rico Brogna or how to pitch him. I can't even remember how I got from the bullpen to the mound that night. I warmed up, prayed, and took a deep breath. Over at first, Jeff Bagwell was holding Jeff Kent on the bag, and Craig Biggio was at second. All I could think was, *God, please let me throw a strike.*

He did. My first pitch was right down the middle and it felt like a huge mental victory. I got Brogna to fly out to left to end the inning. I was done, but I'd made my debut.

BEYOND BASEBALL

Once I got back to Houston, something happened that complicated a difficult season. From the moment I was called up, the team began talking to me about playing winter ball in Venezuela. They'd send players down there to develop and get them ready for the next year in the majors. Normally I would have been there without a second thought—anything to help my chances of staying in the big leagues!

That year, however, I was adamant that I couldn't go. Dennis Stoneman was going to be on trial that winter, and I needed to be there with Sarah and the rest of her family. Some things were more important than baseball.

During batting practice one day at the Astrodome, manager Terry Collins and an assistant coach, Tim Pupura, approached me along with one of the members of upper management. They reiterated that they wanted me to go to Venezuela for the winter and I said, again, "Guys, I can't."

This wasn't a new conversation, but I went over the whole story again, explaining why I couldn't leave my wife while her parents' killer was in court. That's when the upper management guy looked at me and said, "Well, this isn't the OJ Simpson trial."

I just about lost my mind. That was the first time I'd ever really spoken out against authority. I told them, "You can keep the big leagues—I don't need it!" They threatened me, saying that if I didn't play winter ball for them, I might not be on the big league team next year. I stalked back into the clubhouse, as upset as I've ever been. Doug Drabek and Greg Swindell asked me what was going, so I told them through my tears. The demand that I leave the country for months was just so demeaning to me and my family—if there's such a thing as an extenuating circumstance for not playing winter league ball, I'm pretty sure I had one!

Doug went and spoke to management. I was a September call-up, just a rookie he barely knew, but he still stuck up for me. I'll never forget that. He showed me you could still be human and be a top-notch player—you didn't have to put your character on hold if you wanted to play.

The upper management guy has since denied making the comment about the OJ Simpson trial, but I remember his face when he said it. I remember my reaction. How I didn't say the things I wanted to say to him is beyond me. How I didn't punch him is beyond me! Thank God that Doug and Zeke were there for me. After Doug spoke to management, nothing was ever said about winter ball, and the upper management guy never tried to speak to me again.

At the end of the season, I packed my gear and said goodbye

to the Astrodome. Sarah and I left our Houston apartment and headed home to our place in Pulaski, Virginia. We didn't know what the next year would hold. All we knew was that whatever it was, we wanted to face it together.

Being home together after such an incredible season of highs and lows was exactly what we needed. We had the time and space to talk, take walks, and pray. We didn't go anywhere or make any big plans. It turned out that the actual trial of Dennis Stoneman, which was supposed to take place that winter, was delayed until the spring. Eventually Stoneman was found guilty of capital murder, first-degree murder, and related firearm offenses. He was sentenced to life in prison without parole.

Looking back, it was for the best that Sarah and I had that time together without the trial and without me in Venezuela. If we were going to survive the next years of professional baseball, we needed the time to reflect on and process everything that had taken place. Sarah had been alone most of the season, and that winter we rebuilt our partnership stronger than ever. The off season gave us a chance to put that year behind us and look ahead—even though we didn't know what it would hold.

UP FOR GOOD: 1996

The next year, spring training went well, but when the time came to make the final cuts, right before they broke camp, Terry Collins called me into his office and told me they weren't going to take me. That was hard to take. I felt like I deserved a shot—probably the same feeling every kid who goes through spring training feels. *If only they'd give me a chance, I'd show 'em...*

Once again, Doug took me under his wing. As a veteran, he knew what was coming before I did, and he was right there waiting for me when I came out of the office. He told me, "You can pout and bull up, go down there and not pitch well and not get up...*or* you can go down there and show them they made a mistake and earn your way up."

What a confidence boost! I took his advice. I went back to Tucson determined to earn another shot. In my first game I gave up eight or nine runs in the first two and a third innings. Great start, right? I didn't have a good second start either. Fortunately, the Toros manager was Tim Tolman, my Double-A manager from Jackson. He called me in and said, "Listen, I don't care what those people up there told you about not throwing enough strikes, but walks are part of the game. You're a power pitcher and I want you going after these guys."

After that chat with Tim, things started looking up. I went from 0-2 with an infinity ERA to 6-0 and a 1-point-something ERA. It was June 2, and we were playing in Salt Lake City; I was enjoying it, not even thinking about the big leagues. That night I pitched into the 7th inning and I was feeling good when suddenly, for no apparent reason, Tim walked out to the mound to take me out of the game. I was steamed. We were good buddies, but I let him see how mad I was. I stalked to the dugout thinking, *What the hell are you doing?* I wasn't handling things well, sure, but from where I was sitting it was the wrong move to take me out. After that inning I went to the clubhouse and showered and changed. We won the game while I was cleaning up, and as Tim walked through the clubhouse he looked at me and simply said, "Good game, Wags."

Excuse me? That's it? No explanation, and not even a hint? I was still fuming. I thought I should have finished that game. I went back to the hotel as confused and angry as I'd ever been in my baseball career. Just when I was starting to get in a good pitching groove...

Early the next morning, before 7 o'clock, I got a call from Tim. He needed to speak to me right away. I went down to the lobby. He stared at me without saying anything. I still felt lousy, and if he wasn't going to say anything, I was. I started pleading my case. I told him I was sorry about how steamed I'd been, but I wanted to win that game. I was feeling good, I told him, and my stuff was still solid. As I was talking I noticed he was smiling more and more.

Finally he asked me, "You know why I took you out of the game yesterday?"

"No."

"Because you're going to the big leagues today," he said.

"You couldn't have told me that last night?!" I exclaimed.

"Well, I was going to," he said, his smile turning into a wicked grin, "but you were acting so crazy I didn't even want to talk to you."

Ouch—but it was actually a pretty funny situation, too, that Tim and I have laughed about since.

I flew straight to Houston from Salt Lake City. I let Sarah know about the call up and she was packed and on the road and in Houston by that night. We stayed at the JW Marriott right across from the Galleria in downtown Houston. There was a day off before the next game, which gave my wife and me time to relax a little bit. Things felt different this time. A September call up is one thing, but getting called up in June meant more opportunity...and more expectations.

LEARNING TO CLOSE

The first time I walked into the clubhouse, my friend Greg Swindell was the only person there. The Astros were releasing him and giving me his place in the rotation. That was a tough moment; here I was taking my buddy's job, and we both knew it. Greg walked up to me and said how proud he was of me and how excited he was for me. He told me not to worry about anything, that he didn't feel bad toward me. He was as gracious as could be. I've never forgotten how Greg treated me that day, and whenever I need a reminder of what it means to be a man, I picture the way Greg conducted himself in such a tough situation.

Even though I was supposed to start in Greg's spot in a few days, Donne Wall ended up making that start. They decided to have me throw a few innings out of the bullpen before I made my first start. I didn't have to wait long.

We were playing Colorado in the Astrodome on June 8, and Doug Drabek was the starter. He went 2 2/3 innings and was getting hit hard. We were already down 5-1. The bullpen phone rang and the coach turned to me and said, "Hey Wags, go get 'em, kid!" I was still in the starting mode, but I hopped up and got out there. There were two outs and one guy on base, John Vanderwal. I was facing a power hitter, Dante Bichette, but he ended up hitting a fly ball to right field and the inning was over.

I started off the third inning by recording my first major league strikeout against Andres Galarraga...and then giving up my first hit to Vinny Castilla. I pitched three innings that day and had my first Major League at bat—a fly out—*and* gave up my first major league home run to Dante Bichette. That was a lot of firsts, and not exactly the best stat line, but honestly I could not have cared less what happened that day. I was pretty happy with myself for the simple fact that I was pitching in the majors in June and I hadn't made a total fool out of myself.

The next day, Sarah, her mom, and I went out for breakfast, but instead of enjoying my food I got my first taste of harsh criticism. The writers in the newspaper were bashing the heck out of me. They had the expectation that I was going to throw hard and blow away batters, and what they'd seen that first night hadn't impressed them. They were already talking about how maybe I wasn't ready for prime time, and maybe I didn't have the stuff to face Major League hitters.

Because Donne was throwing the ball great, they kept him in the rotation, which meant I stayed in the bullpen. A couple of days later I earned my first win against the Phillies, pitching in relief of

Darryl Kile. Then we went on the road, first to Colorado then to San Francisco. While we were in San Francisco, our closer, Todd Jones, hurt his shoulder. I was brought in to pitch the last three innings and I kept them scoreless.

That was it. After my first save against the Giants, I was a bullpen guy. I never started for the Astros in the big leagues.

Amazing how fast life can change, isn't it? Now, of course, I'm known as a relief pitcher, and it's hard to imagine myself doing anything else. Yet until Todd Jones hurt his shoulder, I was thought of as a starter. That's how I thought of myself. That's how my coaches were training me. That's what the sports writers and scouts expected. And the crazy thing is, for all I accomplished in baseball, I don't think I would have done well as a starter.

In hindsight it's all so obvious. I don't have the type of temperament a starter needs—the patience and craftiness and relentless focus over six or eight innings. I was too hard headed and restless. I wanted to play every day. Heck, I didn't even want to warm up as a reliever! I would toss a couple pitches in the bullpen and then throw 20 to 30 pitches in an inning. I went out there and winged it, really. If you think that sounds way more like a reliever than a starter, you're right. It was truly an example of what some people call a "God thing"—without divine guidance and intervention, I don't believe I would have ended up where I was supposed to be.

Despite my success throughout my career, in every game I ever pitched, I felt sick. I was always keyed up, hyped, breathing hard and feeling jolts of nervous energy race through me. I'd pray behind the mound and say, "Lord help me to be calm and do the best I can. Don't let me make a fool out of myself." Can you imagine having to deal with that every inning as a starter? After pitching in relief, I'd walk into the dugout and everyone would say, "You looked so calm out there." Well, looks can be deceiving! I felt like I was having a panic attack every time I stood on the mound. God might have chosen to put a nice little shield over me to make me look calm, cool, and collected, but inside I was far from it.

In all honesty, I don't think I was as successful as I could have been because I wasn't polished. I could have made things a lot easier on myself. Sometimes I almost looked at my rawness as something to be proud of, but I wish I could have adapted to my role as a closer as easily as some of the other great closers that have pitched. Look at someone like the incomparable Trevor Hoffman—that guy is a machine who clearly made peace with his role early on and then set out to learn every possible trick and tip to make him successful. The biggest difference between other great closers and me was that most of them had time in the bullpen before they became closers. I went from starting pitching to closing, and there was a bit of whiplash in that rapid of a transition. Still, despite my lack of polish, I shudder to think what would have happened to me as a starter! The bullpen was the perfect place for a bumpkin like me to show up and throw as hard as he could!

I was the closer for the rest of that season, earning nine saves and two wins. The point of no return happened on September 21, in the middle of a horrible eight-game road trip to Colorado, Atlanta, and Florida. It was our second night in Florida, the sixth game of the trip, and we had lost every game. This was my first time pitching in Florida and my first time facing the good-hitting Marlins. Doug Drabek pitched awesome that night, 7 2/3 innings of shutout baseball. We were winning 1-0. I was brought into the game in the 8th inning, got three outs, and had to go back out in the 9th to finish it up.

In the bottom of the ninth, I threw two pitches total. The first pitch was up and away to Jeff Conine, and he connected for an opposite field home run. That made the score 1-1. The second pitch was to Devon White, a curveball he hit over the clock for another home run, 2-1. Game over.

I walked off the field, almost unable to believe what had just happened. Doug was standing on the top step of the dugout, watching me get closer. I knew I was in for it, and I deserved to be chewed out, too.

As soon as I got close enough, Doug said, "I don't care what just happened. I want you on the mound tomorrow. You're the best I've seen."

I just about fell over. Even as I write this it's hard to imagine a person so simultaneously full of self-confidence and humility. I had just blown his game—blown an amazing pitching effort when we really needed a win. Doug had every right to rip me a new one. Yet there he was telling me I was the best he'd seen and he'd want me out there closing for him again. His words and his spirit filled me with so much confidence. To have this veteran look past one game to the potential of the rest of my career...well, that changed everything for me. At my lowest point, Doug's words transformed me into a closer with the confidence to do my job and help my team.

Xavier Hernandez was a Godsend that night, too. I had to give a bunch of interviews, mostly to Houston sportswriters. Xavier met me with a beer, a bottle of water, and a towel, and he stood beside me during every agonizing interview. It was the first time I had to stand up and be accountable for getting my butt kicked, but Xavier stayed with me and made sure I was handling it the right way.

For the first time in my career, everyone was watching me fail. I knew I had a choice: to dodge the blame or to watch what I said and then stand behind my words. I knew if I handled the interviews with integrity and accountability I would never lose sleep. Xavier told me, "If we win, it's 'we'. If we lose, it's 'I' or 'me.'" He taught me to never say anything about myself after a win, and to always take the blame after a loss. That's how real teams are created—if you can take the heat of failure and come back stronger, you'll be welcomed back in, but if you run for the hills to save yourself, your teammates will remember that.

When my teammates stood behind me I learned a powerful lesson. I've had many failures in my career, but avoiding accountability for my mistakes has never been one of them, and I can thank my '96 Astros teammates for teaching me that.

CHAPTER SIX

HIGHLIGHT REEL

IN SIXTEEN YEARS of playing major league baseball I've a lot of memorable moments—some good and some pretty bad. I had thrilling experiences on the mound, like pitching Atlanta into position to win the 2010 National League Wild Card. I also had some truly embarrassing moments that just happened to take place in front of more than 50,000 people. Most of these memories, both good and bad, have important life lessons attached to them, which is the way it ought to be. I think we're meant to learn from *everything* we do. When I was a kid, growing up dirt poor in rural Virginia, I never imagined I'd be invited to dinner at the White House or meet my childhood baseball hero, Dale Murphy...just like I never imagined I'd blow a key save on national television. But all those things happened, and now they're part of an incredible highlight reel that I can play back in my mind.

MY MOST EMBARRASSING GAME:
Mets vs. Yankees, May 20, 2006

My single most embarrassing outing happened the day after an exciting win for our team. My first season with the Mets was in 2006. I joined the team as a free agent during the winter, and my signing had high expectations. We were hosting the Yankees at Shea Stadium for an interleague weekend series early in the season.

If you aren't from New York, even if you follow baseball, you may not understand the Yankees/Mets rivalry. Being in different leagues, they don't get to play each other often, so most comparison of the two teams is speculation. But the Yankees have definitely had the better of the rivalry. They're better funded, have all the big-name players, and expect to win. And they usually do.

That year Willie Randolph was our manager on the Mets, and he'd played and coached for the Yankees. He wanted to prove the Mets were as good a team, a better team, than the mighty Yankees. New York fans are intense, knowledgeable, and passionate about their teams. Bragging rights were involved, and the stadium was packed with over 56,000 fans for each of the three games. Not to mention the millions of people who would watch the games or read about them in the papers the next day.

We won the Friday night game, 7-6, and it was a barnburner. The score was tied 6-6 when I entered the game in the top of the ninth inning. I struck out the side—Jason Giambi, Alex Rodriguez, and Kelly Stinnett—all of them swinging. Mariano Rivera came in for the Yankees in the bottom of the ninth, but Paul LoDuca got on base. Then Rivera intentionally walked Carlos Delgado, and David Wright knocked a hit to score the winning run. I got the win and Mariano Rivera, the Yankees legendary closer, got the loss for the Yankees. Our team was fired up, and so were the fans.

The next day we had another packed house. Pedro Martinez got the start for us, and by the eighth inning we were cruising along, leading 4-0. If it had been a save situation, I would have been up and throwing in the bullpen. I probably wasn't the only one who assumed Pedro would stay in for the ninth inning and get a complete-game shutout against the Yanks. So I was caught off guard when, at the end of the eighth, all of sudden I was told to get up and start throwing. I was going to pitch the ninth inning.

When the ninth started, I had the ball. I take responsibility for my actions. I wasn't prepared at all and it showed. I couldn't get a single out. It would have saved everyone time and energy if I'd just turned around and tossed the ball into the gaps myself; it was that bad.

Jason Giambi opened with a single, and then I walked Alex Rodriguez. Two men were on with no outs. Robinson Cano got a hit up the middle that scored Giambi. Miguel Cairo flied out to center. I walked Melky Cabrera and Rodriguez moved to third while Cano went to second. The bases were loaded with just one out. Then I walked Kelly Stinnett and Rodriguez scored. They were beating me to death with my own arm.

Bernie Williams was up next. I hit him with a pitch, sending him to first. Cano scored. Two men were on, there was still just one out, and the score was 4-3. All the Yankee runs were on me. Willie pulled me out and replaced me with Pedro Feliciano. One more run scored and the inning finally ended, but the Yankees had tied it up, and they ended up winning in the eleventh inning, 5-4.

As miserable as it was, I learned an awful lot from that game. It was reinforced to me that I could never take a moment off, which made the 162 games I played that much tougher. I didn't get a mental break. I'd taken on that game, assuming I wouldn't be handed the ball, and that mental mistake cost our team the game.

It also set the tone for the way Willie Randolph and I worked together. It's not a secret that we didn't see eye to eye. I couldn't help feeling like he'd thrown me under the bus that game. Looking back at it from Willie's point of view, I realize he was managing his team against the Yankees, not some random team, and he had the chance to go up 2-0 on them. He wanted to bring in his closer and seal the deal, despite the fact that he had never used me against another team when we had a 4-0 lead going into the ninth. There were bragging rights on the line, which I didn't understand because I'm not from New York. Looking at the situation now, I understand the frustration and pressure he may have felt. But at that point, I was thinking about that game like any other game in the season—what's the best way to win? And it clearly wasn't for Willie to bring in his closer with no warning.

At the end of the day, though, I can't blame him. He wanted to win more than usual, but regardless of what he wanted, *I* should have been prepared. What happened on the mound that night was my fault. I had the ball in my hands and I gave up a four-run lead when it mattered most.

That was my first introduction to the brutality of the New York press. The next day I got absolutely crushed in the papers. It was a nightmare. Everyone was on me. I was embarrassed because it was so public. My name stared out at me from the newspaper racks, and I couldn't turn on the TV without hearing another criticism.

What really humiliated me wasn't that I gave up four runs. I'd given up more runs than that before in an inning. And it wasn't the pressure of playing the Yankees in Shea Stadium; by that point in my career I'd been in the spotlight more than a few times. Those kinds of things weren't easy, but I knew how to handle them. No, what really killed me was that I wasn't ready for that inning. Being unprepared was the opposite of professional. Doing your best and getting beat is one thing, but getting beat when you're only firing on half your cylinders...well, that's something else entirely. I'd failed at my job in a spectacularly public way.

I drove back home to our place in Connecticut. It was the longest drive ever. My dad was there, and I talked to him about how I hadn't been ready. He was a good ear. The last thing he wanted for me was to fail, and he listened until I'd gotten everything out.

Even though I wanted to hide, Dad stayed at home with the kids while Sarah and I went out for dinner and a movie. I thought, "Of all nights to have planned a dinner date!" I felt like every eye was on me, but eventually I began to relax. It was good to be with Sarah. She told me, "You know, it's over. It's not a big deal. *This* is what's important; spending time together." She was right; I'm so lucky to be married to a wise woman.

Humility is almost an intangible, but it's a vital part of being a successful athlete at every level. Just when you think you have the tiger by the tail, he's going to turn around and bite you. Losing that spectacularly was a hard thing to go through. Even now, as I write about this, years later, I feel the emotions. I remember the anxiety I felt that day. I still have scrapbooks of the articles that ran in the papers.

"Yanks Make Sure Billy's Not Hero"

"Wagner, Mets Blow 4-Run Lead"

"Wag the Dog"

"Billy's Subway Series Outings Are Night and Day"

"Mets in Command, Wagner Loses Control"

The whole next day I worried about going to the clubhouse. What would people say? My dad rode to the ballpark with me. He helped give me a sense of security, but I still had to walk through the door myself. When we got to the parking lot, some Yankees players, Johnny Damon and Jason Giambi, came over to talk to me. They knew I had gotten chewed up by the media and they told me not to worry about it. They had gone through it plenty of times in New York, so they knew how it felt.

The last game of the series was an 8:10 p.m. start. Tom Glavine started for us and we were leading 4-3 when I was called in to pitch the ninth inning. You couldn't have written a script any better...or any worse, depending on the outcome! It was time to find out what I was made of. I was nervous, but I knew I was prepared. And when I was prepared, I knew I could perform. For me it wasn't about playing the Yankees that night—I wanted to prove myself to my team, the fans, and the media. I remember talking to God, praying, "Lord I don't care if I win or lose this, but give me the strength to be calm. Just let me be calm enough to do what you've given me the ability to do." I felt like I was visibly shaking. I didn't want to screw up, not after what had happened the night before.

Robinson Cano was up first. I struck him out swinging. Then

Bernie Williams came up and hit a single, followed by Melky Cabrera who also hit a single. Then I got Kelly Stinnett to strike out swinging. With two outs recorded, I felt like the weight of the world had been lifted off my shoulders. The last batter, Miguel Cairo, hit a groundout, and that was the end of the game. I thanked God from the bottom of my heart as I walked off the mound!

Not many people understand how important that game was for me. If I had gone back out and blown that save, the season would have been different. I wouldn't have had any peace, either with the media or in my own confidence. However, being able to ask God to give me the courage to compete the way I knew how, and then giving Him the glory—that brought more peace than I can express. It's tough to find peace on the baseball field when things are stacked against you. I knew God was there with me, win or lose, and He was building me up for something.

Before they got on the bus back to Yankee Stadium after the game, Johnny and Jason came by the Mets clubhouse and called me out to talk to me. They told me how proud they were that I bounced back and pitched well. That was a classy thing to do and it meant a lot to me. The way they acted gave me a sense of perspective that went beyond whether I'd recorded a save or not.

Despite the embarrassment—and because of the embarrassment—I learned a lot that weekend about myself and about dealing with the media. I always wore my emotions on my sleeve, and I'd been taught to stand up and take responsibility for my actions and words. I'd been around long enough to know that what I said could be used or twisted in many different ways, and the next day the media would be in the clubhouse to see if I would defend what I'd said; it was like they were testing me.

I knew I wasn't going to change the way I spoke the truth, but I also knew that more times than not I'd have to defend myself. That became a test of faith. It would have been easier to say, "Forget it, I'm not putting myself out there anymore. I'll just lie or keep my mouth shut." But I would rather stand by my beliefs, even if it costs me popularity. Being a leader means that if you say it, you better believe it, because not everyone is going to like it. That's a baseball lesson that applies to my Christian faith, and vice versa. When I suffer for what I believe, I'm going through a small amount of what Christ endured, and that's not a bad thing.

MEETING DALE MURPHY

Grandma Hall and I loved watching the Braves on TBS when I was growing up. They didn't win much, but they were our team. Back then it seemed like everyone's favorite player was outfielder Dale Murphy. I was no different. Dale Murphy was my baseball hero; I didn't have much growing up, but watching him hit a home run or making a great play would make my day.

I loved how he played the game. He never brought attention to himself, even though he was often the only thing to cheer about! Even as a kid, I noticed how he handled the good days and the bad days. Grandpa Hall showed me that when Dale hit a homerun, he never showed the other team up by pointing or gloating. Instead, Dale put his head down and ran the bases like it wasn't a big deal— like he was just doing what he was supposed to do. Grandpa Wagner also liked to point out players he thought were hot-dogging or looking for attention, and he made it clear that wasn't the way to play the game. That's why I liked Dale Murphy so much. He played the game the right way.

In 2008, when I was with the Mets, I finally got to meet my childhood hero. It was in Chicago, the night before Tom Glavine got his 300th win. Having come up with the Braves, Glavine knew Dale pretty well. He knew how much I loved Dale because we had talked about it when we drove to and from the ballpark in New York. Dale happened to be visiting one of his kids who lived in Chicago the night of that game.

Glavine was getting ready to pitch when Dale came into the

clubhouse to see him. They said their hellos, and then Glavine came over to me and said, "Hey, I want you to meet Dale." I was 37 years old, but I ended up babbling like a little kid. I said something about his back-to-back MVP years in '82 and '83, along with a ton of *ums* and *uhs*! It was pretty embarrassing at the time, and right afterward I wished I could have had a better talk with him. Despite that, however, it was still one of the greatest experiences of my career. Dale had meant a ton to me as a kid watching how the game of baseball should be played, and I knew his character and work ethic had helped shape me.

Fast forward to 2010 when the Braves front office folks came up to Virginia during the off season to see me about joining the team. Bobby Cox and I were talking and I mentioned how much I respected Dale Murphy. Bobby said, "Well you know, Dale's going to be in camp this year…" At that point in my career I didn't care about the money, or records as much as I cared about ending my career as a Brave…and if Dale would be there, even better!

During that conversation with Bobby, I told him that the one thing I didn't like about him was that he'd traded Dale to Philadelphia in 1990. The next year, during a game between the Braves and the Phillies, something happened that caused Glavine, a Brave, to have to throw at the next Philly batter. Dale Murphy came up to the plate. Bobby expected Glavine to throw at Dale, but Glavine wouldn't. He just lobbed it in there. I loved Tom Glavine from that point on. I told Bobby how mad I was so that he would do that to the greatest Atlanta Brave to ever put on the uniform, and Bobby got a little chuckle out of that.

I went to spring training camp in February, and sure enough, there was my hero. I was fortunate to spend hours talking to Dale, just listening to whatever he said about baseball, life, his kids, and anything else. When he'd come to Atlanta, Dale would stop by my locker and talk. As we built a relationship, I learned he was such a genuinely nice guy, and it made me feel good that the person I had looked up to the most when I was a kid was true to form in real life. He was just like I'd imagined. Dale is fun and goofy, just a normal guy who played the game, enjoyed every bit of it, and loves his family. I'm proud to call him my friend.

FIRST ALL STAR GAME AT FENWAY, 1999

Being selected to represent your team and league in the All Star Game is a huge honor, and I always appreciated it. Being named an All Star meant I was doing my job well, and because pitchers are selected by the managers, not the fans, you know it's not a popularity contest. I was fortunate enough to be named to seven All Star teams and play in five during my career. Over the years I got to sit in the clubhouse and hear stories from oldtimers like Tommy Lasorda or get to know current players like Mike Piazza, and I have special memories from every All Star game.

In particular I'll never forget my first All Star game. The 1999 game was held in Boston, and it was my first time back to Fenway Park since my visit during my Cape Cod League days. It was an amazing three days for me and my family. By that time, Sarah and I had our son, Will, who was almost one. Sarah and Will were there, of course, and Sarah's mom and stepdad, Marcie and Jeff Worrell, came up to help us with Will.

At your first All Star Game, everything is "Wow!" Everywhere you turn you're seeing some of the best players in the game. I remember taking my father-in-law in the clubhouse with me. He read the newspaper at a table in the clubhouse alongside Sammy Sosa, Mark McGwire, and Mike Piazza. He told me later that he'd acted cool, but really he was so nervous he didn't know what he was reading.

I couldn't believe I was in the clubhouse or on the field with guys like that. It was a thrill to be able to sit down and talk to players I had only watched on TV or competed against. I talked to Jay Bell and Matt Williams, who I really admired. I was twenty-five feet from

Mark McGwire when he took batting practice, and I stayed for an amazing Home Run Derby.

The night of the game, they did the pregame introductions, calling all the names of the best players for that season. It was incredible to realize that my name was one of them. The National League team stood along the first base while the American League team lined up along the third base line. I remember Roger Clemens stood around third base. He looked at me and sort of tipped his cap, like he was saying "You got here, kid."

What fans and players alike remember most about the All Star game that year was the pre-game introduction of the All-Century Team nominees. The great Ted Williams was driven out to the field in a golf cart, and everyone in the stands went nuts. We players did, too! They parked the golf cart at the pitcher's mound, and we sort of rushed it, gathering around Williams. It was completely unscripted; we were just so excited to see a living legend and pay our compliments and respect to him. In fact it delayed the start of the game, but we didn't care. The teams and former players had to be asked to clear the field area and return to their dugouts. Williams then leaned on Tony Gwynn while he threw out the ceremonial first pitch to his friend, Carlton Fisk. That was a moment I'll be able to see in my mind until the day I die.

The game itself was almost a let-down after the pre-game ceremony. Pedro Martinez was dominating as the starting pitcher for the American League. Curt Schilling was the starting pitcher for the National League, and he gave up two runs in the first inning. By the bottom of the eighth we were behind 4-1. Trevor Hoffman pitched a third of an inning and I was brought in to finish out the inning.

I faced Tony Fernandez first and got him to strike out swinging. John Jaha was coming up, and it just so happened that his buddy, Dave Nelson, was catching. I had Jaha 0-2 and threw a breaking ball to strike him out. As I walked off the field, Dave said to me in a joking way, "I didn't want you to throw that breaking ball. I didn't want to strike out my buddy!"

It's a tradition that when you got to the All Star Game, you buy t-shirts and souvenirs to take back for the rest of your team. In 1999, four of us Astros were selected to the All Star team: me, Jeff Bagwell, Mike Hampton, and Jose Lima. Jeff was excited because he was from the Boston area. He got a limo for all of us and told us to enjoy our first All Star Game. He ended up buying everything for the team. That didn't keep me from doing some shopping of my own, though. I couldn't help buying things for everyone in my family.

The All Star Game itself isn't the most memorable thing for the players—it's the relationships and the experiences you have that weekend. Every time I went to another All Star Game, I learned the lesson all over again: I was so lucky to play with and compete against a group of guys who loved the game and who were fantastic players and people.

PLAYOFF HIGHLIGHTS AND LOW LIGHTS

The post season: it's what every ball club is shooting for from the time they report to spring training until the last out of the regular season. In the 1990s, the Atlanta Braves were the undisputed team to beat in the National League. And in 1997, my Houston Astros met the Braves in the National League Division Series. It was my first trip to the playoffs and it was against the team I'd grown up watching. I was pumped.

1997. The Braves had Greg Maddux, Tom Glavine, and John Smoltz pitching for them, in that order. Talk about a one-two-three punch! We started the series in Atlanta. Maddux pitched like the future Hall of Famer he is. The Braves scored a run in the first inning and a run in the second inning and that was all it took. We managed to get a run in the fifth, but Maddux had a complete game, winning 2-1, and the Braves led the series 1-0.

The next night was the battle of the lefties. The Braves had Glavine going for them, and we had Mike Hampton. The game started out pretty well; the score was 0-0 for two innings. The Braves put three runs on the board in the bottom of the third, but we answered with three runs in the top of the fourth. So far so good; but in the bottom of the fifth inning, the Braves put up three more runs. Then, in the bottom of the seventh, they scored five more runs. That put the Braves up 11-3, and likely put us down 2-0 in the series.

We zipped through three relievers before I finally came in during the bottom of the eighth inning. It was obviously not a save opportunity, but I hoped I could limit the damage in case our bats got hot in the ninth. However, the Braves weren't done scoring. First I gave up a single to Jeff Blauser. Then I struck out Chipper Jones. Fred McGriff then hit a single to left, moving Blauser to second. Javy Lopez was next. He hit a line drive single to left that scored Blauser, and McGriff was able to score on an error by Luis Gonzalez. 13-3. The other two outs came from an Andruw Jones groundout and a Danny Bautista strikeout. Mark Wohlers came in to pitch the top of the ninth for the Braves, and that was the end of the game. When John Smoltz pitched a three-hit complete game and we lost the final game 4-1, it was the end of the series, too.

In 1997 we were just glad to make the playoffs. We won our division by beating a Pirates team who had a losing record. We'd had a playoff drought since 1980, so reaching them was like a "welcome back." We had plenty of pitching, and not much offense, but each year we got a little better.

1998. The next year we made it back. During Game 2 of Division Series against the San Diego Padres, I had my first save opportunity in the playoffs. We were playing in the Astrodome and had a 4-2 lead when I came in to pitch the ninth inning.

Tony Gwynn grounded out to first. Next up was Ken Caminiti, who hit a single between the shortstop and third. Then Greg

Vaughn flied out to centerfield and we were only one out from winning. Bruce Bochy put in Jim Leyritz to hit for Wally Joyner. I was pumping fastballs at him and he was not even close to connecting well, fouling them off one after the other. In an at bat like that, you get to a point where it would make sense to throw a breaking ball. But as I stood on the mound, staring at Leyritz between pitches, my mind flashed back to the 1996 World Series between the Braves and the Yankees. Mark Wohlers had thrown a breaking ball to Leyritz and gave up a home run. I thought to myself, *I'm not going there. He's getting A-plus stuff. Here we go.*

I threw a 98 mph fastball, up and away, and Leyritz hit it. It went straight down the line. It should have tailed foul, but that ball stayed as true as it could possibly stay. In the Astrodome it's tough to hit an opposite field home run, but Leyritz did it. Caminiti scored and we were tied 4-4. After the final out, I sat on the bench wondering, *What in heaven's name just happened?*

The bottom of the ninth started with Dan Miceli pitching for the Padres. Ricky Gutierrez got a single for us to start the inning; then Brad Ausmus laid down a sacrifice bunt to move Ricky to second. Bochy brought in Trevor Hoffman, the Padres lights-out closer. He was pitching to Craig Biggio when Gutierrez stole third. There was just one out. Trevor intentionally walked Biggio to face Billy Spiers, but with men on the corners Billy hit a line drive deep between first and second. Gutierrez scored and we won the game 5-4. What an emotional roller coaster—I had blown a playoff save only to celebrate an amazing playoff win minutes later!

2006. Eight years later, I was pitching for the Mets when we won the NL East Division and went to the National League Championship Series against the St. Louis Cardinals. That Mets team was probably the best team I'd ever been on, talent-wise, at least as far as offense. We didn't have a deep pitching staff. Pedro Martinez had started the season great, but an injury had derailed his second half. By the time the playoffs rolled around, we were relying on Tom

Glavine, Steve Trachsel, and a couple of young guys, John Maine and Oliver Perez, both of whom were pitching in the playoffs for the first time.

The Cardinals had struggled to reach the playoffs, barely squeaked in, and then suddenly began playing like a whole different team. It seemed like every guy in the Cardinals lineup turned into the toughest out in the history of baseball. Albert Pujols held his own, of course, but so did Scott Spezio, Yadier Molina, David Eckstein, Jim Edmonds, Scott Rolen…even So Taguchi; all the guys who hadn't stood out—now we couldn't get them out.

The Series started at Shea, where we won the first game and lost the second. We lost two of the three games at Busch Stadium before returning to Shea to win Game 6. The series was tied, 3-3, and Game 7 was on our home turf.

The rubbermatch was brutally tight. Both teams scored one run in the second inning and it stayed tied 1-1 until the ninth. Endy Chavez made one of the greatest catches—ever—in playoff history in the top of the sixth to keep the score tied. And in the bottom of the sixth, we had the bases loaded with no outs and couldn't score a run, which took away our momentum. We had so many chances to score, but we just couldn't break that game open.

I was up in the bullpen to start the ninth. Aaron Heilman was pitching and he was throwing the ball great for us. Jim Edmonds struck out swinging, but Scott Rolen hit a ground ball single. Then Yadier Molina came up and hit a home run to make the score 3-1. Aaron got out of the inning, but the damage was done. We needed at least one run or we'd be out of the playoffs.

In the bottom of the ninth we were facing Adam Wainwright. Jose Valentin got on with a single, and he was followed by Endy Chavez who also hit a single. Two men on, no outs, and Cliff Floyd came in to hit for Aaron Heilman. Cliff struck out looking, and then Jose Reyes lined out. Two outs, two men on. Paul LoDuca came up and drew a walk. Now we had bases loaded. Carlos Delgado came up to bat and struck out looking.

As the Cardinals were celebrating on our field, I thought, *All this work and all we overcame this year, to lose this way…* That was a tough loss to swallow, and the off-season wasn't any easier. I was mentally and physically fatigued for months, thinking of all we'd worked for but hadn't achieved.

I've been asked if I was angry I didn't get the call to pitch that ninth inning. I wasn't. At the time I hadn't been throwing the ball as well as I should have been. I got a save in Game 1 and a loss in Game 2. My pitches were missing something compared to earlier in the season. It didn't surprise me that Aaron pitched the ninth—at the time he was our best chance to win. To me it wasn't about who the "closer" was, but about making sure our best arm was on the mound. Honestly, it wasn't me. As frustrated as I was that off season, I always felt badly for Aaron.

Those feelings are still sharp. When I played, my emotions were sky high, right on my sleeve for the whole world to see. I can't forget those emotional memories, the anxiety, fear, and excitement all rolled into one. It's odd that one of my most intense playoff memories comes from a game I never played in, yet that's the nature of team sports. You win together and you lose together, and when one suffers you all do. There are a lot of guys in baseball who never get to the playoffs. I was fortunate enough to get there seven times, thanks to my teammates and my managers. And every time we competed as a team, and that's all you can really ask.

2010. My last year in baseball I made the playoffs again, this time with the Braves, the team I loved when I was a kid. What a thrill to take the field for the playoffs with Bobby Cox. It wasn't the outcome we wanted but I got to do something most guys in baseball never get to do; I played baseball in October. There's nothing like it.

Pitching in the playoffs is different. I don't know why. There's a different atmosphere. But I don't remember being nervous, really.

Pitching in New York during the playoffs was probably where I felt the most butterflies. The environment is so hyped up; but I did well there.

My final season I was probably as comfortable pitching in the playoffs as I've ever been. I think I had gone about a month and a half without giving up the run until the very last game of the season, so I was very confident going into the playoffs; I felt healthy and strong. I didn't feel I had overpitched. Bobby had done such a great job managing me. I had actually gone to him to ask him to try to throw me more.

A lot of that confidence may have come from the fact that I knew I was going to retire and that I had done everything, put everything I had out on the field. I knew I was going to do whatever I had to do to win. There was no tomorrow for me. I'm proud of my 2010 season. There was nothing leading up to the season that gave me an inkling of how well it would go for me. I wasn't concerned about losing, I was concerned about winning. When your closer goes out there and says "Give me the ball, no matter what the situation," it means a lot to your bullpen mates, people who usually throw more than you do.

DINNER AT THE WHITE HOUSE

President George W. Bush used to have a "baseball dinner" at the White House each year. He invited active and former players, owners, managers, coaches, media, and other folks in the baseball community. In 2008, when I was with the New York Mets, one of the clubbies brought me a printed envelope from the White House. It was an invitation to a dinner, July 16, during the All Star break.

I looked around the clubhouse to see if anyone was watching me. Even though I'd known the Bush family from my time in Houston, I honestly thought the invitation might have been a prank. Seeing no one lurking or laughing, I found our public relations director, Jay Horwitz, to ask him if it was legit. He assured me it was.

My first thought was how fun it would be to go to the White House with Sarah...until she told me, in no uncertain terms, to forget it. Sarah is very reserved and shy, and there was no way I could convince her to come. There was also no way *I* was going alone, so I called my agent, Bean Stringfellow, and he said he'd keep me company.

And what "company" we shared: Kenny Chesney performed a concert in the Rose Garden; John Smoltz, Kevin Millar, and Cal Ripken Jr. were there, along with all the top baseball historians and writers; and I sat with Tim Kurkjian, the broadcaster from ESPN, and his wife. We were given a behind-the-scenes tour of the White House. While Bean and I were waiting to get our picture taken with President Bush, he called out, "Wags! Hey buddy!" We all had a good laugh; that was the kind of relaxed evening we enjoyed.

I've known President Bush and his family for a while. His father, President George H. W. Bush, used to invite players to come to his office in downtown Houston for lunch. When I was with the Astros, we'd sit around a table and have sandwiches. He'd play a game where he'd pick a letter and we'd go around the table saying the alphabet. Whoever said his chosen letter would win a gift. During one lunch I ended up with a signed picture of President H. W. Bush with Joe DiMaggio and Ted Williams. If you came over to my place for dinner, you'd find that picture hanging on the wall.

Later, when President Bush was campaigning, he worked out at Minute Maid Stadium when he got the chance. I met him in the weight room one day and struck up a conversation. Talk about a guy who loves baseball! After I left Houston, whenever I came to town, I'd look to see if he and Laura were there and I made a point of saying hello to them.

I've performed on a lot of big stages in my life, but being invited to the White House is definitely near the top of my personal highlight reel.

PLAYERS

Please don't get the idea that I was matter-of-fact about meeting people like two former Presidents of the United States and their wives. Nothing could be further from the truth—remember, I was nervous about meeting my boyhood hero Dale Murphy! It seemed like my whole career was like that, giving me unimaginable opportunities to do things I would never have done and meet people I would never have met.

Baseball gave me the chance to meet personal heroes like Dale and Nolan Ryan and Sandy Koufax; those people had an influence on me, and when I met them in person they were even better people that I'd imagined. They worked hard and never made it about themselves, which is a quality that seems to be getting rarer by the year.

I've even had the honor of participating in other player's big moments, like when I got to pitch in Tom Glavine's 300th win in Chicago. Tom is a great pitcher and friend, a sure-fire Hall of Famer, and being able to *play* in his 300th win was a once-in-a-lifetime opportunity.

When I was with Houston I got to play with Randy Johnson, who was traded to the Astros by the Seattle Mariners in 1998 at the July 31st trade deadline. Randy was going to be a free agent at the end of the season, and he made it pretty clear he wanted to pitch in Arizona, close to his home, next season. He got to Houston just as I was coming back from a concussion after being hit in the head with a line drive. When I got back to the team from my rehab assignment, I walked right up to him and started kidding him about being so tall—the guy is like 6 foot 8. I walked out to the batting cage in the Astrodome where he was hitting home runs and I said, "Look at you, you big sandbagger!"

He was very serious and intimidating, but intimidation never bothered me. He was every bit of a full foot taller than me, and he looked down and said, "Easy little fella…"

"*Little* fella?!" I responded. We cut up and had a good time.

It was fun to have another power throwing lefty on the team. We were very similar in our skills, what we brought to the table, but the difference in our height meant our approach to pitching was different. He was already an established pitcher when he came to Houston, but he was becoming even better. He wasn't throwing every pitch at 95 or 100 miles per hour; he was throwing 92 or 93 on a sinker. Then, if he had any trouble, he'd ramp it up and punch out the side. We talked a lot because he was new to the National League and I was able to tell him about hitters he hadn't faced and what I did, how I approached them. Randy likes to take credit for my slider, but we didn't work on it much together. I asked him about it once, he showed me the grip he used, and that was about it.

The first time I was in the playoffs, against Atlanta in 1997, I met "Mr. October," Reggie Jackson; I think he was doing some television commentating. I was always the first one in the dugout for a game. That day I went out and, lo and behold, there was Reggie Jackson, a bat in his hands. I could just tell he was thinking about hitting.

He looked over and said, "Hey, Mr. Wagner! How are you?"

Oh my Lord, I thought, *Reggie Jackson knows who I am!*

I stammered something. Then he said, "You know, I'd like to face you one time. You'd probably show me up 9 out of 10 times, but that *one* time…"

I told him that would be awesome. Talk about an honor—it doesn't get much more humbling than having one of the greatest power hitters of all time say he'd like to take a few swings against you.

When I met Nolan Ryan something funny happened. He'd made his professional debut with a minor league team in my hometown of Marion, Virginia, when he was with the Mets. Naturally, when I met him I said, "Mr. Ryan, I believe you made your debut in Marion, Virginia." Before I could tell him it was my hometown, he said,

"Yeah, I didn't like that place." I didn't know what to say after that! And before I could think of anything, our clubhouse manager said, "Well, that's where Billy's from!" Talk about awkward.

I always loved meeting former players. I loved hearing their stories about the guys they played with and big moments in their careers. It fueled my love of the game as a fan. My own individual games don't jump out in my memory as much and I think that's because I was just doing my job. If I won, even if it was a thrilling win, that was what I was supposed to do. Pitching was the easy part.

Personally, highlights for me were the guys I got to meet or guys I was able to influence. A guy like Braves closer Craig Kimbrel sticks out for me. He was the new kid on the block with the Braves in 2010. I had the chance to talk with him and maybe help him through some things he went through in his first taste of the big leagues.

Craig came to my attention in spring training. He wasn't raw but he had more talent than experience. One of the things that grabbed my attention were the similarities between me and him; the way we threw the ball and other quirky things we did. But mainly, the thing that drew me to Craig was his willingness to learn. He liked to ask questions, he wanted to be one of the best out there. I had the opportunity to reassure him that the same things he was concerned about were the things I was still concerned about. We had a good enough relationship that I could tell him things that other people couldn't and he knew he could trust me. I wasn't going to shortchange him or hold out on him because I was afraid he was going to take my job.

I was like that with all the bullpen guys on my teams, going back to Octavio Dotel and Brad Lidge. I never felt threatened by anyone in the bullpen because I was comfortable knowing that if I did my job I didn't have to worry about anyone else. In my career guys like Xavier Nady and Mike Magnante had stepped up to help me because I didn't have other closers to show me the "secret" to closing.

There really wasn't a secret; it was more the persona, a way of projecting confidence to the other team when you took the mound.

When I spoke to these young guys I'd tell them that closing is not the hardest thing you'll ever do but it will challenge you mentally. You have to learn how to prepare yourself—in the weight room, watching video, going over scouting reports. Those were little things but they all added up.

The fun thing about working with Craig is that Roger McDowell had given me so much leeway with him. Roger asked me to go to the bullpen to work with Craig, and when I came back, I told him, "I changed his mechanics." Roger just said, "Okay." Fortunately, it paid dividends for Craig right away and that was because Craig bought into what I'd told him and worked so hard. He trusted me; he knew I wanted him to do well. I told him that it was a process; he'd always be adjusting, but we all go through it. He had to be himself. He's not me. I wasn't Trevor Hoffman or Mariano Rivera and that's okay. He didn't need to worry about what people outside his team said; he only needed to concern himself with what his teammates were saying. That's who you're playing for.

Talking to other closers always helped because they knew the arena; they knew the frustration and anxiety. I'd see Trevor and other closers out on the mound looking calm and going about their business, but Trevor told me he was feeling the same stuff I felt, he just didn't show it. It was comforting to know that someone else had those same feelings.

To me, having the opportunity to share knowledge and experience with young players is a true highlight—maybe it's the best kind of highlight because that's what it means to be a good teammate.

Meeting people you look up to and having unbelievable experiences in the game is all well and good, but it's the day to day playing of the game—being a good teammate, having successes and failures and learning from them—that really defines your career. I knew then, and it's become even more apparent to me now, that the life

I was living was a blessing, a gift from God to be used for Him. At the time, I wasn't always sure how I was supposed to use the "celebrity" that baseball put on me, but I learned.

I had a lot of lessons that I still needed to learn but God was faithful to bring some great guys in my life, teammates and friends from Baseball Chapel, to help me learn those lessons.

CHAPTER SEVEN

IMPACT PLAYERS

THE TERM "IMPACT PLAYER" is used in baseball to describe a guy who consistently changes the course of a game. You can see it in the way a pitcher approaches a certain batter. Take Albert Pujols, for example. The manager and pitcher—along with everyone else in the stadium—know that with one swing of the bat, Pujols can turn the momentum of a game. So teams make moves based on what a single guy might do, given what he's done in the past and what he's likely to do in the future.

Impact players aren't just for baseball. In fact, they're more important in real life than they are on the diamond. An impact player in life could be a spouse, a parent, a friend, a coach, a pastor—really anyone who consistently changes the course of your life...sometimes without even speaking a word. Albert Pujols can score a run by doing nothing if the pitcher walks him out of fear; the testimony of his life is enough to move the game in a different direction. That's how impact players are in life, too. Other times they get in your face and really let you have it, and because they have built up such credibility with you, you pay attention and grow as a result.

THE IMPACT OF TEAMMATES

Sometimes impact players are literally that: guys I played with who changed me as a person. As a young player coming up through the system, all the way until I retired, I've been grateful to the guys willing to do what I really needed, whether that was taking me under their wing or confronting me with hard things. I know I'm a different, and hopefully better, person because they were in my life.

One of those guys was Lance Berkman, who did me the honor of writing the foreword to this book. He's a tremendous player with a ton of talent and skills, but Lance also has heart and a deep conviction about what really matters. He led his life in baseball as straight and clean as they come, yet at the same time he never made anyone feel judged. It was no surprise that he was voted the "Comeback Player of the Year" in 2011; everyone pulled for Lance because Lance pulls for everyone.

Another guy who made a practical difference in my life was Doug Henry, a pitcher who came to Houston in 1998. He was older than me and had kids of all ages, and he was also a Christian. We talked a lot about situations that came up with his kids and how he handled them. He told me about being tough when he needed to be tough and loving when it was time to be loving; how as a dad he could be hard, but still hug his kids and communicate with them, even if they made a bad decision. During our friendship, Doug let me in on some of the details of his family's life and showed me how it was done. As my kids got older, I wanted to be a father who knew how to make the tough decisions, a father who knew when to say "no" and when to say, "I'm there for you, take a chance!" I never had that kind of father, and guys like Doug stepped up and gave me the model I'd been missing all my life. It wasn't easy to learn how to be a good father while focusing on a stressful job that required me to travel, but Doug, being the "old man," made sure I knew which way was up and then he held me accountable.

When Tom Glavine spoke, he did it in a way that didn't offend people. It wasn't so much that he was "politically correct"; it was that he kept his tongue reined in and only offered his opinion when he needed to. That was a pretty good trick for a guy pitching in

New York City, which is where Tom and I were teammates. I managed to say stuff that bothered everyone over the years, but not Tom. He was cool. And even when he had every reason to blast someone, he wouldn't do it.

Tom used to tell me he wanted to handle things more like *I* did—talk first, apologize later. But I wish I had been a little more cautious, like him. I'm sure Sarah wishes that, too. I was the guy who was willing to say what everyone else was thinking, and the heat would come down on me. Tom and I both stood up for what we believed, and we were respected for it. It's just that Tom had another pitch in his verbal toolkit that I never bothered to develop: tact. In the time I've known Tom I've become more tactful, but I still have a long way to go. I'm trying to learn how to treat people with more diplomacy and care, especially my family, who doesn't deserve to hear the unfiltered opinions I often expressed on the ball field. Looking back, my career and my life would have been a lot easier if I'd met Tom sooner.

When it came to learning what it meant to be a big leaguer, the number of guys who impacted me is hard to count. They taught me about concentration, work ethic, professionalism, and accountability. I'm talking about guys in the Houston organization who reached out to me like Donne Wall, Xavier Hernandez, Jerry Goff, and Craig McMurtry. Guys like Mike Magnante who was there to call my wife when the line drive knocked me out. He and his wife stayed with us at Christmas one year, and my kids call them for homework help. What unites these guys is that they're blunt because they care. They believe in me too much to pussyfoot around the issues. Whether I needed to grow on the field or off, they were always there to teach me how to be more successful. They were never about protecting their turf or trying to get ahead at my expense. Instead, they taught me the true meaning of teamwork: guys united by a single purpose, working hard to make sure everyone else lives up to their potential.

Without these game-changer teammates and friends, I wouldn't have been half the man or the ball player.

BASEBALL CHAPEL

Just as there are impact players, there can also be "impact places." For me, one of those places was Baseball Chapel. Baseball players don't usually have a chance to go to church on Sunday like regular folks, but they do have Baseball Chapel, which is a program of non-denominational Christian worship services and Bible studies in the minor and major leagues. It's a godsend for a lot of guys who are looking for stability in a profession that is far from stable and full of temptations.

Every year I was in the minor leagues during spring training, I'd see Tim Cash, a guy who worked with an organization called Unlimited Potential International (UPI). Tim was great. He knew the game and players, he was a good Bible teacher, and he was easy to talk to. I think he liked me because I was a country bumpkin from Virginia who was low key and had a good heart. Cash was in and out of my life throughout my career in baseball. I'd see him during spring training and when we came to Atlanta, where he was based.

I started going to chapel in 1993 when I was in Auburn, New York. We'd sit out in the stands to have our Bible study. I wasn't really consistent about going to chapel until the following year when I was in Quad City, Iowa; by then I knew how much I needed it in the world of pro baseball.

By 1995 we were in Jackson, Mississippi, where we had another really good chaplain. I was definitely a chapel regular by that time. I didn't want to be another arrogant, look-at-me type of player, taking the gifts I'd been given for granted. In baseball there was a constant pressure to push to be the best and fit in. When you do that, you lose who you are. You lose the perception of what truly matters because all you're looking at is other people's expectations and demands. I knew I didn't want to be that type of person. I didn't want people to look at me and see someone who was entitled, or selfish, or boastful. That wasn't how I was raised, and it wasn't how the players I looked up to most conducted themselves.

Being different wouldn't happen by accident, though, and chapel reminded me of that. The more I went to chapel the more examples I had of guys who were good decision-makers, guys who chose to include God in their entire life, on and off the field. That's what my family needed and it's how I wanted my life to be. Facing the stresses of big league life without God's input would have been disastrous for me. Chapel made what I already wanted into something I could actually do and be on a daily basis.

I loved playing baseball, but I knew from the time I was drafted that God wanted me to be something more than just a baseball player; he wanted me to influence people. All the ups and downs I went through in my life before baseball, in the minor leagues, and even once I made it to the major leagues, were designed to lead me to doing what was truly important—something I'll talk more about in Chapter 10.

You can't go through the minor leagues or the big leagues and have it all be sunshine and rainbows. It's such an up and down life that you've got to find and develop camaraderie. I had to learn to be a good teammate, and before I could be a good teammate I needed to be a good man. It was a process. I learned to say, "This is something God showed me in my life," and I learned to listen when other people said that to me. We were all in the same boat, learning how to deal with the pressures, the expectations, and the temptations.

Chapel was the place I learned God's grace is available, but I have to give Him control and stop trying to handle all the obstacles by myself. Trying to do things on my own, I'd probably fail, but if I went to Him and let Him know I was aware of my place in the scheme of things—that He is God, not me—well, even if I did fail, I'd still survive. During my time in baseball, especially the 1997 and

2000 seasons, things didn't go well for me; I faced conflicts and challenges I had never handled before. If I had looked inward and just said, "I'm a high prospect. I make tons of money, and who cares if I'm good or bad. Look at who I am and what I've done," I would never have become the man I wanted to be. I might have had baseball success—though, I doubt it—but I wouldn't have had life success.

Instead, during all those conflicts and challenges, I asked God for help and wisdom. He delivered, every time. And now that baseball's over for me, I'm more grateful than ever for Baseball Chapel and the way it set me up for the rest of life.

THE IMPACT OF REGRETS

It would be nice if we could learn everything from a positive lesson, but in real life it's often the hard things that teach us the most. No one gets through life without regrets. I wouldn't be human if I never looked back and thought, *I could have done this better.* It's especially true for me, mostly because of the blunt way of speaking I've always had. It's a characteristic that's always eaten at me and led me into situations I regret. There have even been times when speaking the truth got me in trouble because I didn't know how to be honest without being hurtful.

As a kid playing sports, it seemed like everything was either good or bad. I was either the pitcher or the quarterback, where wins and losses were tied to me. There were no "okay" games, no mushy middle ground. Expectations were very high and I had to be accountable. Those were the messages I received, and what went in eventually came out in my own words. Throughout the rest of my career, I held everyone else to that same standard. If a reporter or a teammate asked my opinion, I didn't see the grey area. I spoke just as bluntly as I'd been spoken to as a kid.

Now that *I* have kids, though, it's completely different. I hear how that kind of honesty sounds harsh sometimes, and I remember how it felt to hear it as a 12-year-old. If Will is having an at bat and asks me, "Dad, how was my swing?" and I answer, "It wasn't very good," I often catch myself. He's twelve; I don't need to say that to him. Instead I need to say, "Listen, here's what I was talking about." I guess that's a little bit of sugar coating, but I want to be honest without being hurtful.

I wish I'd learned that lesson early in my career. I don't regret telling the truth, but I wish I had said it with more frosting on top. My clubhouse experiences in Philadelphia and New York were turbulent, to say the least. I regret how I acted at times, but even that has a positive impact in my life now as I try to live the next season of my life differently.

THE IMPACT OF BITTERNESS

I learned a lot about handling criticism and how *not* to be a leader when I was traded from Houston to Philadelphia. When I got traded, it's safe to say I was the most bitter person in the world. I felt totally disrespected by Houston, and I let that eat at me like acid. I took everything the wrong way in that trade, and looking back I know I reacted the wrong way.

It was 2003, and we were battling for a playoff spot. Jimy Williams was the manager, and I was having about as good a year as you're ever going to have as a player, over forty saves and almost eighty appearances. We had just traded Moises Alou for Jeff Kent. Going into the second-to-last season of the series, we had a one game lead over the Cubs for the division title.

We were playing the Giants at home, and Gerry Hunsicker, our general manager, came to the field and told me I would probably be traded. He said that Drayton McClane, the team's owner, didn't know who they were going to trade, but it would probably be me since the team needed to save money. I was in shock, in part because of the timing. We were trying to win our division and go to the playoffs, and the owner was getting ready to trade me while there were still games to be won? It didn't make sense.

We ended up losing a playoff spot, coming in second to the Cubs in the division. A few weeks later, I was sitting at home and I got a phone call from one of the Houston baseball reporters asking whether I'd been traded. I told him I hadn't heard anything, and then I immediately hung up and called my agent, who said *he* hadn't heard anything. Next thing I knew, I got a call from Ed Wade, the general manager of the *Phillies*, telling me I'd just been traded to their team. That was an interesting way to learn I'd been traded, to say the least.

In spite of the strangely timed "warning" from Hunsicker, I was not prepared for the trade at all. I was young and doing my job; I was being paid well, but my salary wasn't ridiculous. To add insult to injury, after I learned about being traded, I never received a single phone call from Gerry Hunsicker or Drayton McClane. Other than my teammates, no one ever called to say, "Thanks for everything you've done. We appreciate it." Now that I've had time to reflect on what happened, I understand that I took their silence the wrong way; I took it personally when I shouldn't have. In my mind, I had done everything I had been asked to do by the organization. I had done my job to the best of my ability and produced good results for them. I thought that meant they owed me something. And maybe they did, but they didn't force me to become bitter and brood about how I'd been injured. That was on me and my immaturity.

Guys like Jeff Kent, Bagwell, Biggio, and Berkman all called to say they'd miss me, but I went to Philadelphia never having heard a word from the Houston front office folks. That's when my bluntness went to a new level. I had an edgy, bitter tone because I just didn't understand why, at the best part of my career—I'd had 78 appearances that year, 86 innings, 44 saves, not taking a day off while trying to help our team make the playoffs—I didn't even get a phone call. It ate at me.

You want to talk about impact? Feeling that bitter taught me a *huge* lesson. I had to learn humility, to learn that at the end of the day baseball is a game and a business. I arrived in Philadelphia angry and acidic. I pushed and pushed to show that I deserved the respect I felt Houston had denied me. I began to turn into someone I didn't want to be...and it wouldn't be until years later that I learned the lesson of bitterness well enough to begin to change the way I lived.

THE IMPACT OF BEING BULLHEADED

I was often approached by the media because I was known as a "good quote." They knew I'd speak my mind, tell the truth as I saw it, and that I would take responsibility for my actions and what I said. That didn't change in Philadelphia. I think some guys on the team felt like I encouraged the writers to talk to me because I wanted the attention. That wasn't the case, however, and very rarely did anyone bring up the times I talked openly to the media about how *well* someone else played.

When I got to Philly, the manager, Larry Bowa, wanted me to step up and be the leader. He told me, "You need to be the guy who gets people going on this team. You need to be the 'hey ho' on the team." That wasn't my style. I'd be direct and tell people, "Hey you need to get your head out of your butt," or, "We're all beat up, get out there and play," but I wouldn't rally everyone around with an inspirational speech.

This isn't an excuse, but I was definitely a product of my raising. Where I came from, if you acted up in the grocery store you got a whipping right there or you heard about it right there. There wasn't any waiting until you got home to talk about your behavior. There were no family speeches to rally everyone. There was a line, and if you crossed it you'd know about it right away.

The Phillies were an up-and-coming team. They weren't far away from where they would soon be, perennial division winners, but at that point they had young kids who needed to learn how to step up and take the bull by the horns. When I spoke frankly about our play, I didn't realize some players took it personally. I just considered it clubhouse talk.

Even though I had two of the greatest seasons in my career, statistically, my time in Philadelphia was overshadowed by one thing I said in the paper about the Phillies going to the playoffs. We were in New York and we had just been swept by the Mets. Jim Salisbury, a writer with the *Philadelphia Inquirer*, asked if I thought we were a playoff team. Here's a portion of the story that ran in the paper the next day, July 1, 2005:

"No chance," was (Wagner's) response when asked yesterday whether he thought the Phillies had what it takes to make the postseason.

"We ain't got a chance to get there right now."

Wagner was standing in front of his locker in the Shea Stadium clubhouse after the New York Mets had handed the Phillies their 11th loss in the last 15 games.

The outspoken closer spoke calmly and never raised his voice. But, in responding to a few questions, he offered a powerful commentary on a team that could be in last place by bedtime tonight.

Wagner, who went to the postseason four times with the Houston Astros, was asked what he believes is missing from the Phillies.

"The know-how to win," he said. "You've got to know how to win before you can start thinking about playoffs.

"There are a lot of reasons to have faith. This ain't over. But anybody who says we have a clear shot to the playoffs right now is fooling themselves. We've got to win."

Would a trade help?

"Adding pieces isn't going to make us any better," Wagner said. "If you don't learn to win and show some fight, it doesn't matter."

Fight?

"We win, we lose, we play tomorrow," Wagner said with a shrug. "There's not that drive. There's not that focus all the time. Good teams find ways to get

it done. The Braves. The Marlins. You don't see them complaining. The Braves were all beat up with injuries and now they're at the top of the division. It's time to quit bickering. We bicker about calls on the field. We bicker about the [size of the] field. It's time to take it upon ourselves and play - concern ourselves with just winning."

We went back to Philadelphia after being swept by the Mets and had a players-only team meeting. The issue was whether it was my place to be saying we weren't a playoff team. The vote was 24-1, and I bet you can guess who that lonely number one was. My teammates thought I was a media whore who just wanted my name in the paper. That wasn't my intention at all. My intention was to *win*. We needed to take these games and this season seriously, because we had a chance—and since it didn't seem like we were, I called it like I saw it.

A lot of the guys in that meeting were friends of mine, but they never spoke up for me or stood behind me. I was left to fight my own battle. I spent the last third of the season in silence. That was my choice because I was bullheaded enough that I didn't want anything to do with them. I was so mad that the team seemed to care more about my relationship with the media than they did about winning ballgames. So I decided to put my head down and do my job. I stopped being there for other guys on the team. I'm sure it seemed like I cared more about myself than the team, but the reality was I'd cared so much about the team winning that I'd burned all my bridges with them.

Now I've grown to the point where it's easier for me to apologize, but back in Philadelphia during those seasons I wouldn't have apologized for anything! They could have shown me something I'd written in my own handwriting and I would've denied it was mine out of spite. That's not who I am now, and it's not who I wanted to be then, but back then when I was backed into a corner, I became someone I didn't want to be.

I believe that season was one of the obstacles God allowed in my life that I didn't handle well. I had to go through it to grow up. What made it worse at the time was being alone. When we went to Philly, Sarah and I made the decision to keep the family in Virginia. Not having Sarah with me was a big mistake. I was enduring one of the worst mental experiences of my life, and it began to affect my relationships outside baseball as well.

After the 2005 season, Sarah and I talked about retirement. My wife and family are everything to me. When I saw that starting to slip away because of the person I was becoming in baseball, the game lost its luster. She helped me see that if I continued to play, she and the family needed to be with me. Sarah is solid. She knew before I knew myself what I could accomplish and who I could be. She understood where I came from, but she never let that become an excuse. She'd tell me what was right or wrong, whether or not I wanted to hear it. That's what I needed. I usually wouldn't agree with her when she told me, but it never failed that when I was driving to the park or driving home I'd suddenly realize, "She's right!"

From that time on our plans were that wherever I played would be where we lived. We'd be a family, because family trumps baseball every time. And to the best of my ability, I was going to be myself, not someone I didn't want to be. There was one person strong enough to be a match for old bullheaded-Billy. God knew that perfect person was Sarah, and he put us together. She was willing and able to disagree with me, in love, and call me out on things. I trusted her. She called *me* like she saw me, bullheadedness and all, and still she loved me.

THE IMPACT OF ACCOUNTABILITY

I was a free agent after the 2005 season. The New York Mets came calling and made me a great offer, and there were other benefits as well. I would have people around me who were supportive, like Glavine and veteran players who were willing to back me up. After what happened in Philly, I needed to know that wherever I was playing, someone was going to have my back. Sarah and I found a house in Connecticut and put the kids in school there, and that's where my life started to get back on track.

However, that's not to say I didn't get into any trouble in New York! I've already talked about the time I was called a racist by a member of the media. As tough a time as that was, and it was really tough, at least I had guys in the clubhouse, as well as other members of the media, who knew me better and backed me up.

Sometimes, though, it wasn't a matter of saying the right thing the wrong way...sometimes I just said the wrong thing, period. One time I got thrown out of a ballgame in New York. I'd already blown the save, and I was trying to throw an inside fastball to Cliff Floyd. It kept running up and in, getting away from me a bit. The umpire, Dana DeMuth, thought I was throwing at Cliff, so he threw me out of the game.

I asked him directly why he was tossing me out. He said, "You're throwing at him because you've blown the save and you're mad." Then he looked at Cliff and asked, "Cliff, was he throwing at you?"

Cliff told him no, but I got thrown out anyway.

I lost my temper *and* my mind. Later on I was so embarrassed that my kids were going to see me on SportsCenter acting like a big jerk. I was crushed about that. I know there are clips of me on the Internet saying stuff I don't want my kids to say and acting in ways that will embarrass them.

Accountability means I have to acknowledge and apologize for what I've done. I can't hide; even with my kids and family, I need to admit that what happens on the ballfield matters to them, too. Situations like that are God's life lessons, the kind of tough love a father gives his child. Without experiences of blowing it, and having to make things right, I wouldn't learn to be the person I wanted to be.

Dana DeMuth may have been wrong to throw me out, but when I started acting like a jerk in front of a packed stadium, I only reinforced his decision. He held me accountable, but I should have held myself to an even higher standard before I got to the point of screaming in his face.

I was raised under pretty harsh conditions, and maybe that's part of why I acted the way I acted. But I've also been influenced by my managers Bobby Cox, Jimy Williams, and Charlie Manuel. They've helped me learn that you're always going to be accountable for what you say and do, so you should take the time to be more careful or gentle. They always spoke to me encouragingly, especially after a bad game. They had a hopeful tone to everything they said, and they made me want to work harder for them because they believed in me.

That's how I want to be with my friends and family. I want to motivate and inspire without tearing someone down. I want to be someone other people want to be around because they know I'll tell the truth without being harsh and inspire them to be better.

These days I'm coaching Amateur Athletic Union (AAU) baseball. I had a kid on my team who's 6'2" and 180 pounds at thirteen years old. One day I got a call from this boy's dad. He told me his son didn't trust too many people, but he had some questions and didn't want to run them past anyone but me. His dad knew that I would shoot him straight and treat him right. It dawned on me that I had earned the trust of that kid because he knew I was truly interested in him. Accountability means that if I say I'll be there for someone, I will. Your negative talk will come back to bite you, and you've got to back up your positive talk with some regular walk. That's what the "impact players" in my life have taught me, and now it's what I'm trying to teach others.

IMPACTED FOR GOOD

Going through the difficult experiences that God allowed in my life, like my childhood, the hard times in the minor leagues, the murder of Sarah's father and stepmom, and my own faults and the difficulties they put me in, all showed me who I wanted to be and why I wanted to be that way. One thing I've learned is that I can only share God's peace with others when I have it myself. And the only way I'll have peace is to rely on God and trust Him to make me the person He wants me to be.

There were many times I stood on the pitcher's mound wondering why God brought me there. I believe now that it was to prepare me for a phone call like the one I received from that kid's dad on the AAU team I coach. I can respond to a kid, whether my own or someone else's, who asks for help. Now I have the perspective to tell a kid that God has a purpose and a plan for his life.

I can't know with 100 percent certainty what God's purpose is all the time, but I know that God is good. We take life a step at a time, and sometimes God gives us a glimpse of what He will do through us. We're all going to make mistakes and be judged—I know that from plenty of personal experience!—but how will we handle it? Do we become more selfish and defensive, or do we turn to the Lord and say, "I can't handle this. I need Your guidance. I need Your grace."

I look back and wish I had been more willing to apologize and been a better teammate, husband, father, and person. Yet as time has passed, all the conversations I'd had with Sarah, with fellow believers, and the time spent reading the Bible have begun to sink in and make more sense to me. Life hasn't been all smooth sailing, but over time I've become better equipped to handle tough times. The impact players in my life have helped me realize I don't need other people patting me on the back and telling me I'm good. As great as you can become at baseball or anything else, you have to know who you really are, so that when there's nobody there to pat you on the back, you can look yourself in the mirror with integrity. That's when you need to answer these questions affirmatively: Did I do my best? Did I learn? Did I help others along the way?

By 2008, I was enjoying life and the game in a brand new way.

And part of that came from an forced time-out due to an injury. It's funny how God knew that was just what I needed. I shouldn't have been surprised, since He'd used injuries before to give me a breather, personally, professionally, and spiritually. He was about to do it again.

CHAPTER EIGHT

KNOCKED OUT

THE PHRASE "KNOCKED OUT OF THE BOX" refers to a pitcher who is knocked out of the game, usually because the hitters are showing him he doesn't have his best stuff. But all sorts of things can knock a pitcher out of a game or sometimes an entire season. Injuries are usually the main culprit, and I've had my fair share of them over the years.

Though painful, I believe my injuries have been some of the times God has taught me the most about who I really am and what really matters. Just like the "impact players" who helped me become more like the man God wants me to be, injuries have had a positive impact on my life. I don't believe there is such a thing as "wasted" time. Whether I was on the field or rehabbing from an injury, I could learn from the experience. No one wants to be injured, but how we respond to the time away can make a difference when we come back.

In baseball, just as in life, sometimes things happen for no apparent reason. The key is to look for the reason and keep trusting and working.

1998: KNOCKED OUT ... FOR REAL

It was July 15, 1998. Sarah was a little over eight months pregnant with our first child, Will. We weren't expecting any drama, especially for me—I figured any "drama" would be dealing with the delivery and our newborn. The last thing I expected was to be hit with a line drive while standing on the pitcher's mound.

My Houston Astros were playing Arizona. The game happened to be on ESPN, and I knew Sarah was at home in Houston, watching the game. It was a tight ball game. We were ahead 8-7 in the ninth inning when I came in to close it out. I gave up a hit to Matt Williams and then struck out Travis Lee swinging. Then Kelly Stinnett came up, and on the first pitch he hit a line drive right back at me. The baseball hit me on the left side of my head and I dropped to the dirt.

I never felt the impact. I was lying on my back and my legs were moving, involuntarily. I could hear everything being said around me. The most disturbing comment was, "Oh my God, he has blood coming out his ears."

All I could do was keep repeating, "Tell my wife I'm okay."

As I was wheeled off the field on a stretcher, I moved in and out of consciousness. When we passed through our bullpen, my good friend, Mike Magnante, was there, and I grabbed him and said, "Make sure to call Sarah and let her know I'm okay."

The hospital, with all the tests, CAT scans, and MRIs, was a blur.

I was in the hospital when I first saw video of what had happened. I was still wearing my uniform, lying on a bed, and Dave Labossiere, the Astros trainer, was in the room with me. The TV was on, and sure enough a clip from the game showed the ball hitting off my head and ricocheting into the stands. I was glad to be alive.

The team had returned to Houston after the game, and I managed to talk the doctors into letting me fly back home the next day. Sarah and Mike met me at the airport, but I couldn't walk. I had a terrible case of vertigo. Mike came on the plane, I put my hands on his shoulders, and I walked behind him with my eyes closed, all the way to the car. I kept my eyes closed the entire ride home. Because of the vertigo, I was constantly nauseous and could only eat Jell-O. If I moved too quickly I'd get sick. I never had headaches, but the vertigo lasted about two weeks.

I sure wasn't in a baseball frame of mind. The doctors told me they didn't know how long that would last, and they sent me to a physical therapist at the Houston Medical Center who worked with equilibrium and balance. Every time I turned my head too quickly I threw up, which wasn't a good sign for a relief pitcher!

The therapist used a device to help me regain my balance. I walked into a two foot by two foot circular tube. The floor rotated, forward, backward and side to side while I stood there, trying to maintain my balance. I went through a couple of weeks of that all while thinking, *This is not working*. But it did help. It just took some time.

Sarah and I were still waiting for Will to be born, so I had more on my mind than just getting back to playing. I think that's why I didn't get too caught up in "poor, pitiful me," because there wasn't time to think about that. Besides, my experience had taught me that times of adversity could build character. It wasn't about what happened as much as it was about how I responded. My goal was to build on the things I could control, and to trust God no matter what happened.

As I rehabbed, I counted my blessings. Number one, I could have been killed by that linedrive. God blessed me enough to protect me. My Grandma Hall said I had angels around me to protect me, and I guess she was right. Number two, I was excited that I would get to see my son being born. Sarah's labor was induced right before I left for a rehab assignment, so I was able to be there when Will came into the world on July 29, 1998. I might not have been there if I hadn't been injured. Viewing my injury and rehab that way, I didn't become resentful. And my childhood helped me be more relaxed about injuries, since I learned at a very early age that there were things I couldn't control and would have to endure. Playing baseball and being successful were icing on the cake—God had blessed me more than I could ever imagine.

When I got hit in 1998, I wondered if I would get back to baseball. I heard people say that some players never come back after being hit. I had to look inside myself and listen to what I knew. I knew that God had given me the strength to get through it and I needed to fight the temptation to feel pity for myself. I guess it's a blessing that I'm so hard-headed that I don't give in to that type of thinking.

I had also heard people say that being apprehensive was normal once you get back on the mound—it would be hard not to be more tentative given what had happened. When I was sent to rehab in Jackson, Mississippi, my number one thought was that I wasn't going to pitch scared. I thought I'd thrown a fastball away when Kelly Stinnett pulled it up the middle and hit me, but what I didn't realize was that it was an inside fastball he had shot back up the middle. Since I didn't want to be afraid of throwing fastballs away, I threw one to every hitter I faced. I pitched to my fear, and overcame it, even if it was with the wrong pitch!

When I got back to the big leagues, Houston had just traded for Randy Johnson. My first outing was against the Phillies. It wasn't a trial for me, because I'd already overcome my concerns in the minor leagues. That's not to say the "what if" wasn't in the back of my mind but, when that happened, I'd tell myself, "I'm going to show you." I wasn't going to give in to the temptation of fear. I knew I had to compete and battle. It helped me get out there and do it. There were times when I stood on the mound and my catcher would call that fastball away...I'd take a deep breath before throwing it—but then I'd throw it with everything I had.

Later that year, we were in Cincinnati and Scott Servais hit a line drive back at my head. I caught it. I remember holding it in my glove and then walking to the back of the mound and taking a deep breath. It seemed like after that there were more line drives back at me, but I caught them and made plays. Eventually, I just got back into the flow and slowly forgot about being hit.

I was always much more afraid of giving in to my fear than I was of being hit, but that wouldn't be the last injury challenge I faced.

1999: TORN FLEXOR TENDON

I'm pretty sure I tore my flexor tendon on September 21 in Pittsburgh when I came into the game in the eighth inning to face Chad Hermansen, Al Martin, and John Wehner. I struck out Hermansen on three quick pitches, but on the first or second pitch to Martin, I felt a *pop*. My arm swelled up immediately. I walked Martin, but Wehner grounded into a double play to end the inning. I came off the field and told my pitching coach, Vern Ruhle, that I felt something pop in my elbow. The trainers said, "We'll treat it." It was close to the end of the season, and I was only used sparingly.

We made the playoffs that year, and I ended up pitching in Game 1 of the NLDS against Atlanta. I had a 1-2-3 inning. We won the first game, then lost the second game. We came back to Houston for the next two games. My elbow was killing me. I was given a cortisone shot, but it didn't help. I tried to suck it up and pitch— they got me up to warm up during those last two games, but I never had to go in. The Braves won the final two games and we were done for the season.

In spite of the injury, I had a really great year. I led all Major League relievers with a 1.57 ERA and placed third in the National League in saves with 39, which set an Astros record. I was even awarded the Rolaids Relief Man of the Year Award. But my arm was hurt and I knew it. I was told to take the winter off, then rehab and my arm would come back. I was told it was tendonitis. I remember being in the training room during spring training and Gerry Hunsicker told me, "All you've got is acute tendonitis! Everybody's got little tears—you need to suck it up and play."

"Alright," I said. So I pitched in spring training and almost thirty games in 2000. My stats were okay, but it got to the point that I couldn't get anybody out. My arm was killing me, and I couldn't take it anymore.

I was taken out of the closer role. We were in San Francisco and they brought me in to pitch the sixth inning. There was a pop up down the right field line that fell in for a hit. I had a terrible outing and I told Hunsicker again, "My arm is killing me. I need to get something done."

He said, "You should have let us know. You should stop being such a tough guy." I love and respect him to death, but he and I really got into it when he said that!.

I went to see Dr. Louis Yocum, and that's when he discovered a partial tear in the flexor tendon in my left elbow. That explained a lot. Hard-headed me; I'd been trying to pitch all season, just nursing my elbow along, doing what the trainers told me to do. Up to that point they were just doing treatments, ice, and electric stimulation. The treatment didn't do anything but cause more frustration. When Dr. Yocum finally diagnosed the tear, I was relieved. It could be fixed.

Dr. Yocum did the surgery in Los Angeles. When I woke up, he asked me to squeeze his hand. I was able to squeeze his hand with my left hand and I knew I was better; good to go—all I had to do was start rehabbing. Then it was just a point of going through rehab, which went really well. I've always been a stickler for doing what the trainers and doctors say. If they told me not to throw a ball hard, I didn't. I never took that chance. But when they said it was time, I didn't even think about that. I just let it go. I was on the disabled list from June 21 until the end of the season. I actually started playing catch on September 1st, then rehabbed all the way through the winter.

After the surgery, I asked my agent to set up a meeting with me,

Gerry, and the two doctors from the Houston Astros. It wasn't a pleasant meeting. In fact, I was as rude as I could possibly be. I had a big cast on my arm and I screamed at Gerry when he came in the room, saying, "Does this look like tendonitis to you?" And I used some pretty bad language, too. It was on. He screamed right back at me and I screamed at him.

I yelled at the doctors calling them quacks. I was upset that my injury had gone undiagnosed and virtually untreated—that the staff had told me to suck it up when there was something seriously wrong.

I was especially angry that Gerry tried to blame me by going to the newspapers and saying that it was my fault I hadn't been treated, and that I hadn't told anybody I was hurt. That infuriated me. I became that redneck always lurking inside me. Believe me; I said what was on my mind. This whole thing went on for about thirty minutes and then Gerry said, "Tell the doctors to leave." The doctors left.

When we were alone, he turned to me and said, "Hey, I love you. I'm sorry."

Now, the good thing about Gerry was that you could speak your mind and really get into it, but when it was over, it was over. He knew how to handle players in those tense moments that escalate. That meeting was necessary for us to clear the air and for me to say my piece. My arm was already hurt and I felt they hadn't helped me; in fact they may have made it worse. But what was done, was done.

That experience taught me that I needed to become even more vocal about injuries and issues that could affect the length or quality of my career.

When players would come to me and tell me they were hurt and didn't think they were being listened to, I voiced my concerns. I became known as outspoken, but I felt it was important. I knew I had to take responsibility for my health, and that naturally led to advocating for other guys who needed someone to back them up. I know the team cared about me—when I was producing. Let's face it:; professional sports is a "what have you done for me lately" kind of deal. And when you're not producing you're not on their radar.

That was a real world lesson for me and it changed the way I handled my career. This isn't any different from what happens in careers outside of baseball. When you work for a big company, your value to the company is measured against what you can provide for them. If you're not producing in a factory, in a company, or on a baseball team, you better be looking over your shoulder because someone is always there to take your place. I was fortunate to learn that lesson when I did—early enough to make a difference. I knew it was my responsibility to protect myself, health-wise and financially. In a strange way, tearing my flexor tendon early on helped my career.

2001 - 2008: BUMPS AND BRUISES

In 2001 I tore up scar tissue pitching against the Dodgers. I threw a pitch and it felt as if my hand was on fire. After what happened the year before, the Astros overreacted and put me on the 15-day disabled list even though the next day I was fine, playing long toss. Essentially it was a 15-day vacation. I asked them to send me to Triple-A Round Rock so I could get some work in. It was kind of silly; I told Gerry Hunsicker the day after it happened that I was fine. But they decided not to take a chance and in hindsight I appreciate them taking care of me.

After that season I had three good seasons with Houston. In fact in 2003, I pitched a career high number of innings and broke my own saves record, earning 44. It was because I loved pitching for my manager, Jimy Williams. I love that guy. I was also named Pitcher of the Year by the Houston chapter of the Baseball Writers Association of American (BBWAA) and got the Good Guy Award.

But the following season, 2004, I was traded, and when I went to Philadelphia I was pretty beat up. I had every injury possible, shoulder strain, groin pull, you name it. I couldn't stay healthy for nothing. I actually had trouble staying healthy from 2004 until I retired in 2010. My first rib up by my left shoulder kept popping out. After I pitched the trainers would have to pop it back in. I had two stints on the disabled list while I was in Philly; I had a groin strain in 2004 early in the season and a strained left rotator cuff toward the end of the same season.

After my first year in New York, 2006, I started having back problems, spasms and pain. That's when I started thinking 'I'm getting old.' I started missing games. We had a big series with the Phillies that season. I was at our home in Connecticut and lifted a door in our closet when I had a spasm in the middle of my back between my shoulder blades. I fell onto my knees; I was in so much pain. I could barely get to the ballpark. I had two days of caudal shots—like an epidural—cortisone shots, whatever they could do until the last day of the series when I was finally able to pitch.

One time during my last year in New York, I had a back spasm that was so bad I took four cortisone shots and three caudal shots in the same day just to be able to try to pitch. It was miserable having to do that to try to get through a game, and there was always the possibility that you wouldn't have to pitch anyway.

When I got to Atlanta in 2010, I talked to Takashi Saito. He also had back problems. I was pitching well and felt good but I was concerned about fatiguing my back. His personal trainer came in and did an acupuncture treatment on my shoulder and back. His guy really took care of me and I was able to get through the season without any problems.

TOMMY JOHN SURGERY AND THE METS

Between the time I tore my flexor tendon and 2008, I had my share of bumps and bruises, including torn scar tissue in my hand, a shoulder strain, a groin pull, rib trouble, a strained rotator cuff, and painful back spasms. It wasn't until 2008, however, that I experienced an injury that would truly test me...and nearly end my career.

Throughout the winter between the 2007 and 2008 seasons, Sarah and I had discussed retirement, together and with the kids, but it never felt quite right. But at the beginning of 2008, we started talking about retiring with my agent. I always wanted to be the best player I could be, and when my body started to give way to injury it was pretty clear to me that it was getting close to the time to make a decision. We were leaning very heavily toward retirement and had even mentioned it to some close friends.

It was a strange year, to say the least. I was having a solid season, living up to the expectations that I had for myself. I made the All-Star team and was throwing the ball almost as well as I had earlier in my career.

The first few years in New York there was a good deal of turmoil between me, my manager, Willie Randolph, and the team. Willie was replaced by Jerry Manuel in the middle of the season. I liked Jerry. I felt he had a good relationship with his players. Before he became the manager, I enjoyed talking to him one on one. He had a good spiritual relationship and I enjoyed hearing what he had to say. I always felt like he understood me. When he and I spoke after I injured my arm, I took what he said in such a negative way, but that was part of the way I always reacted. I know he didn't intend it that way.

I had so much to learn. When I look back now, my injury was a blessing. The time I had to take off for Tommy John surgery and rehab were absolutely essential for me so I could step back and get my head back where it needed to be.

We were playing in Florida when I hurt my arm. It was the end of July, and Sarah and the kids were going to meet me in Houston after the Florida series so we could celebrate Will's birthday in Houston with our friends, the Maganate's. I had told Mike that I might retire at the end of the season, so they were meeting us there to watch me pitch and to hang out with us in Houston.

We had three games in Florida; I got hurt in the second game of the series. I was called in for the ninth inning. I was all warmed up and threw the first pitch to Alfredo Amezaga and felt it immediately. It was a pain similar to what I felt when I tore my flexor tendon; a sharp pain, like lightning, followed by a deep, dull ache that seemed to go away. I finished the inning and then told them I was hurt. The coaches and trainers said I might have some tendonitis and decided to give me some days off. That was on a Tuesday night. We had an off day in Houston on Thursday and that Saturday, the second day of the series, I played catch. I didn't feel great, but I was okay. I got in the game that night and pitched terribly. I couldn't get a soul out.

That's when they shut me down. I was put on the disabled list with tendonitis, so I started rehabbing with Chris Correnti, a minor league rehabilitation trainer. We did all sorts of treatment for two weeks. Then I was sent to my first rehab in a game with Double-A Binghamton against the Reading (PA) Phillies.

It went great. I punched out the side, was throwing 96 miles an hour and I was so excited to be throwing really well. On the ride back to New York, however, I couldn't lift my left arm. I was supposed to join the team in Pittsburgh, but I couldn't even play catch. I had to rehab another two weeks. At this point I spoke to Moises Alou to ask his advice. I told him I knew I was hurt but that they wanted me to throw. I was concerned I was going to hurt myself even more, and that my career might be over. He told me I needed to find out what exactly was wrong. Maybe it was something that could be fixed—at least I'd know soon rather than later. Moises was right. I needed to throw and get it settled one way or the other.

I spoke to my manager, Jerry Manuel, and said I wanted to throw. We had a split double header at home in New York, Sunday, September 7, against the Phillies. In between the two games we set up a simulated game. I couldn't have thrown any better in my first inning. I threw thirteen pitches and struck out three. I was dirty; normal as could be. As I started to walk off the mound, the Mets

pitching coach, Dan Warthen, said, "Wait, you need to throw another inning." I wasn't sure why, since all they need me for is one
inning, but I stopped and sat down a minute to rest and then
stepped to the mound again.

When I started warming up I could tell that something wasn't
right. I threw a pitch to Gustav Molina and the ball landed at his
feet. My elbow felt like it had exploded and I heard a snap. It was
my arm. The pain was so intense that I was in tears. I didn't really
need an MRI to tell me what had happened—I tore the medial col-
lateral ligament in my left arm, and my flexor pronator, a muscle in
my forearm, too.

Jerry Manuel walked up to me, put his arm around my shoulders
and said, "You've had a good career."

At the time I was in such pain that I couldn't respond. *What did
he just tell me?!* Later, however, when the pain was under control, I
was furious. I thought, *What? How could he say that?* It was kind of
funny since I thought I'd probably retire after that season by choice,
but once I got hurt it was a different matter. I heard people saying
I was done, that my career was over, and that I would never make
it back at my age—now comments like *that* got my competitive
juices flowing! Being a competitor I wasn't going to allow anyone
else to tell me when I was done. I would let *them* know when I was
done.

Like so many other pitchers the last few decades, I got ligament
transplant surgery, usually called Tommy John surgery. Mine was
on September 9. The typical rehab for major league pitchers is one
year. Some guys come back more quickly, other guys take longer,
but no one seemed to think I would be back. That doubt became a
huge motivation for me.

During the offseason, I didn't hear anything from the Mets. I
finally got one call from the general manager, Omar Minaya, asking
me how I was doing and telling me not to worry about coming to
spring training. I asked Chris Correnti to work with me. He set up

a workout schedule that I could do on my farm. He and I would talk once or twice a day. Chris found me a rehab guy to work with, Lloyd Givan at The Performance Place in Charlottesville. Lloyd nearly killed me! We worked so hard, and he gave me so much confidence. I told him, "I'm going to be back and way better than anyone expects me to be."

Once a month, I'd drive to the Mets facility in Florida for a week of workouts. Then I'd go home and do my workouts for another three weeks. I was already throwing, but the Mets didn't like it. They told me I was throwing too hard and told me to stop throwing in March. By April, seven months after my surgery, I was throwing 150 feet with no problem. In mid-April, I threw off the mound for Guy Conti, the Mets rehab coordinator and my bullpen coach from the previous season. I didn't have any problems.

In May I went down to Florida for another week, and I was still throwing great. At that time they told me they didn't want me to come back again until late June or early July. They wanted me to just rehab and see where I was at by that point. Will and Jeremy came with me to Florida. They loved it; they had a great time getting to see all the young guys. We'd be at the ballpark all day and they got to see me go through my process of throwing. I kept getting stronger.

The Mets didn't want me to get in a rehab assignment too early. By this point they had Francisco Rodriguez closing for them. We did something we called the tenth inning. They would play a game, and right after the game ended I'd go in and throw a tenth inning against our team. That was going well, and I began to wonder when I'd be ready to pitch in a real game.

Out of the blue, however, they told me to go home for ten days. For the first seven days I couldn't pick up ball, and for the last three days I could play catch and get into my program. That was a confusing order, but I did it. I could tell, though, that I was a game or two away from coming back—I was way more ready than my team thought I was. I said, "It's time to talk to Minaya and set up when I could come back." Chris talked to Omar because they had Frankie there. Omar was concerned; he had apprehensions about me coming back. He questioned whether I really wanted to come back. I was furious. I drove to New York from Virginia and had a meeting with Minaya, Jerry Manuel, and my agent. I said, "I'm ready. Bring me back or trade me."

I made my return debut on August 20 against the Braves. It had been eleven months since I had surgery and I was throwing 96 to 97 miles per hour. I was hitting my spots. But on a personal level, the best thing was that the game really slowed down and became enjoyable to me. When I look back now, my injury was a blessing. The time I took off for Tommy John surgery and rehab was absolutely essential for me so I could step back and get my head where it needed to be—and so I could enjoy the game of baseball like I had before.

A renewed appreciation for the game wasn't the only benefit. The time away led me to a much stronger faith. I searched myself and determined who I was and what I wanted to be. I believe God gave me another opportunity to be on the pedestal of professional sports in order to be a beacon for Him.

The Mets were out of the playoff race that year. Seven days after my comeback, I was traded to Boston. I was nervous because I still wasn't sure how long my arm was going to hold up. I didn't want Boston to give up a lot to get me, only to have to stop pitching if my arm went bad. I called Terry Francona, who was managing the Red Sox, to tell him that I wasn't sure what I could give him. But he told me they'd been scouting me since I'd been rehabbing. He thought I could help them. Sarah and I talked it over for a long time and it came down to the last minute before we made the decision.

The move to Boston was a great move for lots of reasons. Boston was where I went to my first big league game during my summer in the Cape Cod League. I played my first major league All

Star Game there. The fans are great and the Red Sox were headed to the playoffs. To top it all off, I got reconnected with Tim Cash, in Baseball Chapel.

That's when I really started asking questions., *Who am I influencing? What am I doing here on this mound, throwing a baseball? What's the purpose of this?*

Maybe it was because I'd almost hung up my glove for good, but I was able to reflect on my sport and my career. So much of baseball and professional sports is being around guys and getting caught up in what they're wearing, the places they're going, what they have because you want to fit in. But that's not who I wanted to be. I came into baseball because I wanted to play. It was something I could do and I wanted to be good at it. And at the end of the day, I wanted to give to others. All the other stuff else took away from what God put me there to do—which I knew was going to last far beyond the final pitch of my final game.

When Atlanta came calling during the 2009 off season, it was like was God was saying, "You have had this whole career and this time off, so show me what you've learned. Show me how you've matured in your life to help somebody else."

Everything I'd ever worked for in baseball and in life came to fruition in Atlanta. I had a great manager, great teammates, I was healthy, I was playing for the team I loved when I was a kid, and was in a position to do what I really wanted to do: ,and that is to help other people.

CHAPTER NINE

RETIREMENT

ALL GOOD THINGS COME to an end.

2010 was the time for me to bring my 16-year career to a close. Believe me, I know how fortunate I was to be able to call the shots and go out on my terms. It's rare in life and in sports. Just a few years earlier it could have been a different story; I had to have major surgery just to be able to have a normal life, let alone play baseball. Athletes have a limited shelf life. The games and practices take a toll on your body, and recovering from games takes longer.

The decision for me wasn't primarily about my body, though. The wear and tear on my body was nothing compared to the wear and tear on my family. The love of the game is one thing, but as my wife and kids got more and more used to life with a husband and father who was gone all the time, I had to look in the mirror and ask, "Is this what I'm all about?"

Physically I could have played another year or two, but after spending time on the disabled list and seeing what my family dealt with when I wasn't there, I knew I needed to be home for good. Their lives were basically on hold while I pitched. I was continuing to chase a dream that had already been fulfilled.

It's hard for people to understand why I didn't stay in the game a bit longer, since I was so close to reaching John Franco's record of 424 saves for left handed pitchers. When I say that wasn't a driving force for me I get some strange looks, as if I'd quit running a race just before the finish line. It took me fifteen years of playing professional ball to realize that as much as I loved the game, my family had sacrificed enough. Overstaying my welcome as a professional athlete wouldn't be worth it just to have a plaque on a wall or a line in some record book.

That's not who I am. I'm a husband and father before I'm a baseball player. I wanted my choices and my life to reflect that.

MAKING THE DECISION

My last year in baseball was one of my favorites. I simultaneously felt more relaxed and more focused because I knew there wouldn't be a tomorrow—another year—for me.

Spring training was great, as always; it's one of the best times of the year anyway. The Braves held their camp in Orlando at a great training complex on Walt Disney World property. I got down there a bit early and took my time settling in. When everyone arrived, I told a few people that I thought I'd retire at the end of the season, but they didn't pay it any mind. I'd say, "This is it for me," but they'd reply, "Yeah, yeah, Billy, sure…" Nobody took me seriously.

I'm not sure how serious *I* was, to be honest. Maybe I was just trying out the idea to see how comfortable I was with it.

I remember throwing an early bullpen session to Brian McCann before the rest of the team reported to camp. My stuff was awful. That wasn't a surprise to me because my spring training pitches were usually pretty bad, but Brian looked concerned. "Don't worry about it," he said, "You're okay. It's no big deal." Typical Brian; he's a really good guy, and he was trying to make sure I didn't get down on myself.

I told him, "This season is probably my last hurrah."

"Hey, you can't worry about that bullpen session," he replied.

I wasn't; if I retired that season, it would be for entirely different reasons.

Despite feeling relaxed and focused, it was still difficult preparing for that final season. Getting ready for 162 games is hard enough, but I'd changed teams. They had expectations, and so did I. I didn't want to let anyone down. Fortunately the new clubhouse I walked into was the Atlanta Braves clubhouse, the team I used to watch with Grandma Hall. I felt so comfortable, as if I'd always played there.

In the clubhouse there were two rooms of player lockers, a smaller room where most of the veteran players had their lockers and a larger room where the minor leaguers, non-roster invitees, and some of the bullpen pitchers had their lockers. Mine was in the smaller room, in the same row as Chipper Jones, and I could slip away from my locker and right into the training room and workout area whenever I needed to.

I didn't know what the atmosphere would be like in the clubhouse, and more importantly I didn't know how the guys on the team would perceive me. Would they believe what they'd heard or read about me, or were they going to get to know me? I had played against a lot of these guys for years and they'd probably heard some of the stories about me from Philadelphia and New York. Some of the guys told me they'd heard I was a "hard ass."

Once they got to know me, thought, they realized I was just as hard, if not harder, on myself. They saw me in the weight room, or running, or talking to the younger pitchers and working out game plans with Brian. The guys saw that I got to workouts early and left late, and I think they realized I was more than the sum of the media stories about me.

But it wasn't all work. There was a lot of laughter and camaraderie in the Braves clubhouse. You could rag and rip on everybody. The first day I walked in wearing jeans, cowboy boots, and a cowboy hat, someone said, "Hey Tex." We had a great group of guys, from the youngest players to the coaches and manager.

We broke camp feeling good. We had a decent spring training record: 17 wins, 12 losses. Those numbers didn't really matter; we knew we had a good team. I was more eager to get to the regular season than usual, eager to get on with what I knew would be my last year in baseball.

Thirteen games into the season, we had an 8-5 record; not bad, but not great. Then the bottom dropped out. In late April we lost nine games in a row. It was still early in the season, but we dropped to fifth place in the standings. No matter how many games you have in front of you, you do not want to have to climb out of a hole like that.

Trade rumors began flying. That was the last thing I wanted; I was very happy in Atlanta. "Well shoot!" I thought, "I like it here. I don't want to go anywhere." I was pretty sure I'd be one of the guys they'd trade if they needed to look for help. I was concerned that if that happened, I would end up who-knows-where, and probably as a set-up guy. That was not the way I wanted to go out. I really wanted to get to 400 saves and go to the World Series as a closer. If I didn't, it wouldn't be the end of the world, but it would feel like the end of the world if I ended up as a middle-inning setup guy on some last-place American League team.

Sarah was back in Virginia and I needed to talk everything through with her. I told her, "I'm just telling Bobby I'm retiring at the end of the season. That way they won't trade me because all they'd get would be some draft picks!"

In the end I announced my retirement almost accidentally. During that nine-game losing streak we had a seven-game road trip. We finished up with four games in St. Louis. Before the last game of the St. Louis series, I was shooting the breeze with the Braves radio broadcaster, Jim Powell, in the visiting dugout. We were talking about all sorts of things, and he probably asked me how long I thought I'd keep playing. I told him that this would be my last season. I didn't think any more of it, but Jim mentioned my decision to retire on the air during his broadcast that afternoon. Carroll Rogers, a baseball reporter for the *Atlanta Journal-Constitution*, was back in Atlanta, listening to the broadcast.

The next day we were back in Atlanta, and I decided to tell Bobby. When I got to the ballpark, he and I were in the food room, just off the clubhouse, all alone. I turned to him and blurted out, "I'm planning to retire at the end of the season and I just thought you should know."

"No, you're not." That was classic Bobby.

I assured him I was serious, however. I wanted them to be able to plan for that season and the next, but I also didn't want to get traded. After he and I talked, I went about my usual pre-game business. I thought Bobby would probably tell Frank Wren, the Braves general manager. I'd talk about it with Frank and that would be it.

Carroll came to my locker before the game and asked me about my decision to retire. I assumed she'd heard the news from Bobby, and I confirmed it for her. She then wrote a story, which was posted online during the game. By the end of that night's game, all the other team reporters had read the news online.

When I returned to my locker after the game, a pack of reporters was waiting for me. I'd pitched the save that halted our losing streak, so I figured that's what we were going to talk about. Instead, one of the guys said, "We hear you're planning to retire at the end of the season." I was surprised by all the interest. It hadn't occurred to me that anyone would care I was retiring. I thought I could just throw my last pitch—a fastball, of course—and ride off into the sunset.

In the end, having my decision to retire out in the open early in the season took the pressure off of me. I didn't have to consider and reconsider. I made my decision and continued to feel confident it was the right one. I could relax and enjoy my final season, and that's exactly what I did.

CONSIDERATIONS

Lots of guys retire, only to return either the following season or even later.

My idea of retirement is that finished means finished.

Like I told McCann that spring, I don't believe the decision to retire should be based on a good or bad outing, or even a good or bad season. You have to make your decision based on your ability level, your health, how much you still want to compete, and—the most important reason—what's happening in the rest of your life.

Health-wise, I was feeling drained and beat up more and more after games. Even if I didn't pitch, I would often get up and throw. The older you are, the longer it takes to recover. I knew I wasn't bouncing back as quickly as I used to, and I knew that would affect my ability to compete.

More than my health, though, I thought about my family. They were always on my mind that final season. I was starting to miss too many activities, too many smiles and touches. Will was already going to middle school and Jeremy was moving closer. I wanted to be there for that transition. When I was a kid, moving around constantly, I didn't have my father around to talk me through tough times or explain the things dads explain. I wanted to be there for them. Compromising or losing my family relationships because of my career simply wasn't an option.

I said my family came first, and it was time to walk my talk. They certainly benefitted from my experiences as an All Star pitcher and the material possessions my career provided, but they sacrificed a lot along the way—like stability and friendships and time together—and no amount of money in the world could buy that back.

A childhood spent following dad around to different ballparks sounds glamorous, as does being a mom who doesn't have to work outside the home or worry about finances. If you're looking solely at the physical things, maybe that life is glamorous. All I know is that my family wanted something more, something intangible that we could only find by making the simple but hard choice to be with each other more.

Baseball and my family were on either end of a balanced scale, and that final season my desire to be with my family began to outweigh my desire to compete. I had always enjoyed the competition of athletics, but I become much less tolerant of the expectations and criticism that comes with playing at that level of the game. The cost to me and my family—the things we were missing—didn't outweigh the benefits.

Sarah and I had talked about retirement for years, so she knew it was on my mind. When I made the public decision so early in the season, I think she was relieved to know when that part of our journey would be coming to an end. She put up with way too much loneliness and waiting over the years, sitting by the phone after a game or dealing with sick children alone.

More than once I thought about how Sarah was alone when she got the call telling her that her father had been murdered.

She was ready for me to be home. To her credit, she never asked me to retire. Sarah always wanted it to be my decision and she didn't pressure me. She never wanted me to have any regrets about my career, and thanks to her I don't. Not many people are as blessed to have someone that would sacrifice so much and never complain. I am, though, and she's a blessing far bigger than baseball could ever be.

HOME

I've been asked many times whether I had second thoughts.

The answer is...of course! It's only natural to wonder what would have happened if I'd kept playing. What I realized was that I'd have those second thoughts no matter when I retired. Choosing one path always closes down another. So I had a few doubts, and a few questions, but I knew I'd had enough.

My actual transition into retirement was pretty smooth. I like being with my family, so having lots of time with them and planning my day around *their* schedule instead of the other way around was a treat. I had a plan for the first few "innings" of my retirement, too. Besides helping raise our four children and working on our farm, I was going to help run our educational foundation, which I'll tell you more about later. Some guys retire without a plan and discover there's only so much golf they can play or "hanging out" they can do before they're bored. Believe me—I haven't been bored in retirement!

After so many years focusing on baseball, I had no idea what day-to-day life with four children would be like. I discovered it's unbelievably busy and that Sarah's ability to make our home life look so easy is near miraculous.

For the first few months everyone was still getting used to the fact that I was home full time. It was as if they thought, Who's that strange man who looks like Daddy? The kids would get so excited that I was actually home every time they got back from school or practice that they'd jump up and down. That really reinforced that I'd made the right decision about leaving baseball to spend more time with my family.

I began contributing to our community, too, helping coach my son's 6th grade basketball team, our under-13 AAU baseball team, and Jeremy's Little League team. All our children, except our youngest, Cason, are playing sports, and Olivia dances as well. Now that Cason wants to start playing, Sarah and I look at each other and say, "How?" Sarah tells me I need to be a better time manager, and she's right. I'm such a high stress guy, running around trying to get things done quickly when I have plenty of time to do it. She keeps me grounded about things like that and walks me through my day so I can focus. She's really amazing—it turns out I can't really function, in baseball or in life, without a good manager.

One thing Sarah and I planned for was how I might feel during December or January after retirement. That's usually the time of the off-season when pitchers start thinking about tossing the ball, shaking the cobwebs out. Most ballplayers will tell you they get the itch to get to spring training in January, especially if the team has made exciting moves like picking up a big free agent or something like that. And it turned out I *did* have that itch the first year, but we'd talked about it and I expected it. And honestly, I was so busy with our kids and their activities that I didn't have time to think about it for very long. There's nothing like setting the lineup card and keeping stats for a bunch of kids to keep your mind busy; being involved with my children's teams has helped me stay involved with baseball, but in a way that connects me to my family. I love it.

Retirement came down to this: I had something more important to do than play baseball.

I never pretended that playing baseball was changing the world or making life better for other people. It was entertainment. Everything I got from baseball was personal: an identity, respect, and self-satisfaction in doing an elite job at a high level. Of course it provided for my family as well, but almost any job can do that. No, God showed me over the years that my baseball career was for a short season and a specific reason—He wanted to use me to bless other people long after I'd thrown my last pitch.

Baseball gave me an opportunity to support our Second Chance Foundation, our churches, and people I know who are struggling. Those are the things that are most important to me. I feel far more satisfaction from making a real difference in my community than I ever felt from getting a save.

Baseball is fun to play, but I always pressured myself to be the best. The game brought out the selfishness in me. That had a cost to my family. My schedule controlled my life *and* my family's life. Trying to prove my worth, day in and day out, and putting in those extra hours in the weight room or throwing those extra pitches...well, I saw that change me into a person I didn't really want to be. Every family man has to make tradeoffs, whether he works a 9-to-5 job or is a professional athlete. I made some tradeoffs and asked my family to do the same, but after sixteen years it was time to take less from them.

It was time to give them more of me.

WILL HE OR WON'T HE?

Even though I said I was retiring and never backed away from that decision, there was, and still is, speculation about whether I was serious. I guess folks love a good mystery.

I didn't do any special rehab work on the oblique injury I got during the 2010 playoffs because I didn't intend to play baseball again. I didn't work out the way I normally would have during the off-season to prepare myself to play the following year; I never picked up a baseball except to throw with my sons. I never gave any interviews or even hints about a comeback. It was a one-hundred-percent done deal as far as I was concerned.

During the off-season, I got a couple of texts from former teammates about coming back to pitch. Brian McCann and Peter Moylan both asked me if I was getting ready for spring training. I never gave it a thought. But heading into spring training 2011, it started to seem as though no one believed I was serious about retiring, even Major League Baseball. I never got retirement papers.

All winter long I was still on the Braves 40-man roster, even going into spring training, which led people to wonder whether I was planning to come back. The reason behind that was sort of complicated...and it wasn't because I wanted to pull a reverse Michael Jordan and try for a pro basketball career!

It all had to do with my contract. When I signed with the Braves in 2010, I had a one-year contract, but there was a clause in it that if I finished fifty games, an option for a second year was automatically picked up. Once I hit that number of games in 2010, my one-year contract automatically became a two-year contract. Because I retired in the middle of what became a two-year contract, the Braves couldn't drop me from their 40-man roster without having to pay me the money that would be due me under the contract. We eventually settled the issue when I waived my 2011 salary and agreed that the Braves would have exclusive rights to me until the end of that season if I made a comeback.

It was a moot point to me. I knew there wouldn't be a 2011 season, or any season after that. Despite the confusion, despite the questions and speculation from the media and other players, despite the fact that I probably could have played longer if I had wanted to, I didn't have a doubt in my mind that I had retired, once and for all. When I finally signed my name to the bottom of my retirement papers, I was happy to do it.

Besides, I had to sign those papers fast so I could get to my daughter's dance recital and plan for the next 6th grade basketball game. My days of standing on the mound were over, and a whole new adventure was just beginning.

CHAPTER TEN

ON DECK

WHAT'S NEXT?

That's the $64,000 question about retirement. Baseball had planned my life for me since I was a teenager. It was like I was standing on the pitcher's mound, looking at a young player I'd never faced before swinging a bat in the on-deck circle. I knew what sort of stuff I threw, but I didn't know what the young player was capable of. It was a new situation I couldn't totally prepare for.

My decision was final, but what would happen next was not. I knew *why* I was retiring, but I wasn't sure what I'd *do*. I knew I wasn't going to relax and play golf every day, as if I'd "earned" that sort of privilege for working so hard as a pitcher.

Nothing against the game, but it rarely seemed like real work. There's a lot of hard work involved in being prepared, yes, and there's work in playing, but at the end of the day it was still a game. It's not back-breaking labor, and it isn't some tedious job in an office or factory for a low wage. The amount of money baseball players make versus the work they do is crazy, and I was determined to remember where I'd come from and why I'd been blessed with a good arm and ample finances.

When you're pitching it's easy to become self-centered because everyone is catering to your needs. Sarah would say to me, "You're so selfish," and I couldn't see it. It took a long time for me to see that even when I was home with her and the kids, I wasn't really there. I wasn't present for them. I was thinking about baseball; what I needed to do to get ready, how I could get better, what I wanted out of it. I became very self-absorbed. When guys don't have someone to help them break out of that selfish prison, they end up "needing" to spend their time and money during retirement on themselves.

For me that wasn't something I wanted, and it wouldn't have been an option anyway, even if I had. With four children and a working farm, I knew I was going to be busy. But just like facing new hitters, figuring them out and how to succeed against them, I've had to learn about new opportunities in retirement that I never expected. Despite all my accolades on the mound, this next chapter might be the one I'm most excited about sharing—because it's about the lasting impact I'm being called to make in my family and my community.

KIDS

I don't know if there's anything more important than parenting. You can give your kids all the presents in the world, but what they really need and want is your presence. One of the best things about being home all the time now is that I'm getting to see my children grow up. Each one is unique, and I love watching them explore the things that they're passionate about.

My oldest son, Will, loves baseball. He puts high expectations on himself and we talk about that a lot. He thinks he's supposed to be better because of what I've done, so we make a conscious effort to let him know he's his own person and he needs to find his own path in life. He's also an emotional guy; his heart is on his sleeve. He's a lot like me in many ways, including size. He's a good fielder and a good hitter, too, but he's a little fella. The guys on his travel team are anywhere from 5'5" to 6'3", and he's 5'2". At 15, he's one of the youngest on the team. He hits .307 and does really well, but he thinks he should be hitting the fences on a high school field. He's not vocal about it, but he's rarely satisfied with how he's doing. We try to encourage him to be his age; he's right where he needs to be, and now's the time to just enjoy the game and not make it a job. I've told him he's *way* better *and* bigger than I was when I was his age. Being there for Will during this time of his development means the world to me.

Then there's Jeremy, our spark-plug. He's thrives on playing and is always improving. He doesn't feel pressure the same way his older brother does. He catches, pitches, and he loves to close. When I'm coaching he'll tell me, no matter how we're doing, "I want to do it. I'll close it out." He's only 13, but he has a desire to develop the closer's mindset. He's not the greatest at shaking it off if he loses, but he never shies away from wanting the ball in his hand during the big moments. When things don't go his way, it's a project for me to keep him calm and not let his emotions run wild. He got so emotional when a teammate made an error or had a bad at bat that I finally had to bench him for a game. I told him he needed to be a good teammate and learn how to be positive to every single player before I ever thought about putting him in a game again. That was miserable for me, but from that point on the light went on for him. If things don't go well he handles it better than before. I keep reminding him that winning or losing isn't going to change his life.

We've learned to be very strict with both boys about their expectations. They've been exposed to how tough it is to play and stay in the major leagues, so they make baseball at their level much harder. Kids their age don't necessarily need to hit or take grounders every single day—it's my job to get them to be kids when they're acting like adults too soon.

When they get up in the morning, they've got the MLB Channel on, watching game highlights. We live in Virginia, but they have friends who are Braves fans, and because I grew up a Braves fan and played for the Braves, my boys still like Atlanta. Like all kids, they'll play outside and pretend to be different players; it varies from day to day, but I see them acting like Chipper or Prado or McCann. It makes me chuckle, knowing I played with those guys and my kids want to be just like them. It's fun to sit back and see that.

Olivia, 10, is probably the best athlete in the family. Movement comes easily to her, and she has so much coordination and flexibility. She's probably stronger than the boys were at her age, and she's not afraid to get out there and hit the baseball or mix it up when the boys are playing basketball. Sarah recently coached Olivia's basketball team and they won the championship. Olivia's real passion is dance, though—ballet and hip-hop. When she's not at dance class, she's practicing her routines at the house. I'm so impressed by how confident she is. She and a friend performed in a school talent show and she's really fearless. She puts herself out there and doesn't care what other people think. She's as much on the go as the boys are. I don't do as much with Olivia as I would like to because I'm tied up with the boys' teams. Sarah will pick her up from dance class and bring her to the field. I'm already thinking about how to add a new "pitch" to my arsenal: regular Daddy-daughter dates. I want to show her I'm as interested in the things she loves as I am in the boys' sports.

Kason is just 6. He goes to school now, but my first year of retirement he was home all day several days of the week. We were buddies. I'd take him to the pitching barn and throw him batting practice a couple times a week. When I went to the ballpark early for one of his brothers' games, he went with me. He loves riding on the four-wheeler when I drag the infield. Kason isn't playing team sports quite yet, though not from lack of training by his older siblings! He says he'd like to play football when he gets the chance, but we'll see about that. I know he's going to have a thing or two to teach his sister and brothers as he gets older. No one knows more about being "the little guy" than the youngest of four kids!

The longer I'm retired, the more I realize that it's all about paying it forward to the next generation. It doesn't matter who you are and what kind of work you do—if you have kids, you're busy with them and their activities. You're juggling their likes and dislikes and all the things that go on in their lives. And you don't do it just because you should; you do it because you love it.

My mom moved up here from Tennessee recently, which gives us another "bus driver" and another pair of loving arms for the kids. We've all grown even closer since I left baseball. I think about a 45-minute talk I had to have with one of the kids after a touch Little League loss. That kind of talk happens all the time now. If they have a difficult practice or game, I'm available to talk them through it.

Time with your family is literally priceless. I wouldn't trade it for a World Series ring.

NONESUCH FARM

After living in cities during my career, when it came time to settle down, Sarah and I decided to come back to Virginia. We got lucky. We live in a small town near Charlottesville, Virginia, in the Shenandoah Valley, right at the foothills of the Blue Ridge Mountains. It's a beautiful part of Virginia, with lots of rolling hills, trees, and streams. We bought a house with 60 acres in 2000 called Nonesuch Farm and we didn't see any reason to change the name. Over the years we've added some more acres to it as land has come up for sale, and we love our little patch of Appalachian heaven.

Because it's a working farm, there's always something that needs fixing or doing. Everyone pitches in, including our kids. As they get older, they get more chores and more responsibility, and that's a wonderful change from a life spent on the road, living in hotels. Of the 200 acres, about 150 of it is pasture for our several dozen cows and our 14 alpacas. Our farm manager, Brad Cogan, and his two sons, do most of the work on the farm. Brad runs the day-to-day operations with the hay and cows, but if I'm not working around the house I'll go out with him and work on the farm or in the hay field.

I'm doing more coaching now than farming, but my first year of retirement I loved to spend time on the tractor mowing hay. Now if we have one of those rare days with nothing going on, we all get out in the yard and mow. About three or four years after we bought the farm, we started our cattle operation. We raise Black Baldy's, which are beef cattle. In the spring we'll get around 15 calves, and we usually take eight to ten of them to sell. You can probably guess that a few of those cattle end up on my grill, but we also have a great vegetable garden where Sarah grows organic herbs. Sarah was a town girl, but she's making up for it now.

I swore up and down that I'd never have a farm because it's constant, never-ending work. I grew up working in hay fields and hated it. But when I was away from it for long enough, I realized I missed it. I like being outside, and my kids do, too. It gives us something we can do together. And if I ever get tempted to relax and take up golf, the farm lets me know that's not an option!

These days I'm lucky if I catch a couple innings a night of a baseball game. I'm so tied up with what's going on around our house and in our family that I don't have time to sit around and play the shoulda-coulda game. And that's the way life *should* be.

COACHING

In truth I haven't really retired from baseball so much as changed venues. As any other parent/coach can vouch for, being a baseball dad is intense. Of course it's a completely different level of the game, but it's still baseball, and it's fun for me to be able to bring all the experiences I had during my career to the field with me. Not everyone who played major league baseball would want to coach, and even fewer would want to coach at such a basic instructional level, but it's something I enjoy. After decades of being so hard on myself, I have a ton more patience with the kids I coach.

I coached a couple of travel teams in 2011, the season after I retired. Some of the kids on my teams went to the Miller School of Albemarle, a private school in our community, but the school didn't have a junior varsity baseball program. I talked to the school's athletic director and the varsity coach about starting a JV program, but we didn't know if there would be enough kids interested. After we held an assembly, we ended up with ten kids who committed to the team. I helped build a baseball field so we'd have a decent place to practice and set up a ten-game schedule against other schools in the area. We did everything from scratch the first year, but my assistant coach, John Llewellyn, and I are committed to helping those players make the jump to varsity.

One day the varsity coach for Miller was watching me workout with the kids. He went back and told the headmaster of the school he didn't realize how good I was with children. When the headmaster told me that story, I said, "Why wouldn't I be? I don't know much, but one thing I know is baseball, and the other thing I know is kids—I've got four of them. And for the last six or seven years of my career I was *playing* with kids!" That led to me coaching not only the JV team this spring but also the varsity team as well.

Seriously, coaching is incredibly rewarding for me. Knowing I'm making a difference in kids' lives is important; after all, coaches have made a huge difference in my life. Still, coaching my own children can be tricky. For example, if I tell the kids on my team something, I get, "Yes sir! Yes sir!" But my own kids look at me and ask, "What? Are sure you know what you're talking about?"

The good part is that I'm still Dad to them, not a former major leaguer, and that's just how I want it.

I work the whole team the way I work my own kids. We practice to be perfect and we drill a lot of fundamentals. I'm a tough coach. We've done ground ball drills for an hour if we need to. I try very hard not to be biased toward my own children. If I have to get on my son, I do it. If I have to take him out of the game, I do it, just like I would anyone else's son. When parents see that, they know I'm not favoring my own children. I've occasionally had some parents tell me they're tired of seeing the Wagners play wherever they want to play. But I explain that until their kid is ready to catch or pitch or whatever, I'm not going to put that boy in a pressure-packed situation that demands skill he doesn't have. Once I explain that, they usually understand and respect the decisions I make. I don't have to speak to the media after games any more, but the community can be just as tough!

Recently I told Sarah that I probably would have retired a lot earlier if I had realized coaching was going to be so gratifying and enjoyable. These kids aren't learning about baseball so much as they're learning about life. If you don't hustle on my team, I pull you out. If you don't listen to the coaches, I pull you out. If you back talk, I pull you out. It's not about winning or losing—it's about the character of that kid. I want each kid who plays for me to have a character defined by hard work, listening, learning, and respect. Those are lessons that last a lifetime, not just nine innings.

When I talk to kids, especially those who are small, I explain to them that they're in charge of the way they think. They have to trust that God has a plan for them and it doesn't have anything to do with their size. Think about David in the Bible, who killed the giant Goliath when he was just a kid. It's about how much heart they have to fight the good fight. Each time a kid pushes through a barrier after someone says they're too small and can't do it, they come out the other side stronger. When things really get tough, I tell them, they can always count on God.

I can see now that my whole life, from growing up to playing professional baseball, has been God's way of giving me the ability to empathize with and encourage children and young adults. The cliché is that kids are the future, but that's so true! I invest a lot of time in coaching, mentoring, speaking to FCA groups, and that sort of thing. When I can help a kid transform his character, I know the world will be a better place for years to come. That kid will do better in school, relate better to his parents and siblings, and someday be a better husband and father to a whole new generation. Isn't that what it's all about? I truly believe that my career as a pitcher was a set-up to what I'm meant to do for the rest of my life.

SECOND CHANCE LEARNING CENTER

In Chapter Four, Game Changers, I told you about my best friend, Erik Robinson. In 2005, I started the Second Chance Learning Center with Erik. Second Chance is a nonprofit foundation focusing on education in southwest Virginia, where both of us grew up. Erik and I decided our foundation should be like a fastball: focused and direct. There are a lot of worthy causes out there, but we keep our attention on two things, education and intervention. I know from personal experience how important those can be. Not every kid who struggles in school will go on to college if they get help, but shouldn't they at least be given a chance? Erik's background is in social work, and he knows firsthand what a major difference early, effective intervention makes in a kid's life.

Second Chance works with programs that are already in place through the local school systems. We partner to provide counseling, tutoring, and mentoring for tweens and teens in Bluefield, Eric's and Sarah's home town, and Tazewell, my hometown. Second Chance also offers scholarships to students who want to go on to college and grants for local classroom teachers.

I gave the seed money to start the foundation, but its ongoing funding comes in large part through sponsors, donations, and fundraisers. We have an annual golf tournament, and in 2011 we put on our first "Second Chance Rocks the Two Virginias," an all-day country music concert that benefitted Second Chance. It was held at Mitchell Stadium in Bluefield, West Virginia, and drew about 18,000 people—pretty good for our first year. It's important to us to make Second Chance a natural part of the community that people support and buy into. It's a grassroots thing, by the people and for the people, and we're proud to be part of it.

Two students who went through our program at Second Chance and received scholarships to attend college have already graduated with four-year degrees, and ten more students from our program are currently in college on scholarships. When I spoke at a banquet recently, one of our students who was attending Virginia Commonwealth University also spoke. This student had a severe anxiety disorder that had affected his ability to learn. We were able to get him help to manage his disorder. He graduated from high school and went to VCU on a Second Chance scholarship. He delivered a five or ten minute speech that was tremendously inspirational. Seeing that type of outcome is what keeps me motivated. Intervention isn't a free ride; it's making sure a poor kid from a poor town doesn't end up causing trouble with a 12-inch Bowie knife.

Running a nonprofit is one of the challenging new hitters I'm learning to face. In addition to fundraising, getting community support and buy-in, and finding the right staff, we still have to manage everything. Even though Erik and I are best friends, we've had disagreements over decisions that we've had to work through. We're always honest with each other, and we've learned that we can separate our friendship from our organization because at the end of the day, everything we do is for the kids. By raising the level of education in the communities Second Chance serves, we can raise the likelihood that corporations will relocate to the area or expand. Second Chance is playing a key role in developing an educated workforce in southwest Virginia.

There are days when I wonder if all the details are going to drown me, but one minute spent thinking about the kids and how they're counting on me makes me swim even harder. If you live in Virginia, or just care about helping kids there have a chance to succeed, I'd sure like to see you find out more about our foundation. Just fire up Google and punch in Second Chance Learning Center.

PERSONAL GROWTH

As you can tell by now, I'm a passionate guy. At this point in my life, I focus that passion on three things: my family, education (both on the baseball field and in the classroom), and God, since everything I do depends on His strength and guidance. When I left baseball, I realized that if I was going to pursue those passions and be successful in the next season of my life, I needed to pay attention to a couple of personal issues that needed cleaning up. I knew I couldn't be as good a father or a coach if I kept some of the habits I'd picked up playing ball. Interestingly, both had to do with my mouth.

Sarah used to say to me, "I know you've been in the clubhouse too long." Boy oh boy, I could cuss with the best of them...or the worst of them! I was working in an environment where a lot of guys cussed, and I did, too. It's not something I'm proud of; for me it was just everyday talk, but I realized it wasn't the kind of talk my family needed to hear every day.

Being away from baseball has helped. I might not change to the point where I never cuss, but I would sure like to display more self-control. I know that if I really don't want to cuss, I can trust God to help me change. I regret I didn't try to clean up sooner. When I met Lance Berkman, he never cussed, and I thought that was the neatest thing. I heard guys say he didn't have any backbone or stupid things like "I can't trust a man who doesn't cuss," but I was always impressed by his ability to say what needed to be said without relying on curse words.

We all have moments where we don't say or do the right thing. As a Christian, I'm not supposed to be perfect, but I am supposed to use my moments of imperfection to confess my faults and failings and inability to make it on my own. Cursing is a way to deal with stress or anger, but it isn't the only way. We're made in God's image, and He's competitive, too. He wants everyone to be His son and daughter. He wants us to make the right choices. He wants good things for us. God knows we're human and we're going to fail from time to time, but He's always pulling for us to win.

As for me, there are still days when my wife says, "Oh my goodness, it's like you never left baseball." I always remember what Tim Cash told me, that God knows my heart. There's no doubt in my mind that He knows my heart and that I'm forgiven when I cuss. Even though I talk about developing self-control, I know it really takes Spirit-control. I can be a slow learner, but I'm trying, and I know that even seeing me fail and try again is a good model for my kids.

QUITTING CHEW

Quitting chewing tobacco was pretty high on my to-do list of things to accomplish for my first year of retirement. It wasn't going well at the start of this book and now, many months later, it ain't goin' no better! It's still on the to-do list. Sarah has been great. She hasn't pressured me even though I know she wants me to quit.

Obviously I can't use dip when I'm coaching, but occasionally I'll have one in before practice. When the kids ask me about it, I say, "Do as I say not as I do," on this subject. It's not a great answer, but it's really all I've got. I tell them that they should learn from my experience and never start using tobacco. I try to explain it's not cool. I try to explain how hard it is to quit.

This is a battle I fight every day. I tell myself I don't need it, but then when I get in a pressure situation or I'm bored, I'll put in a chew. I might only keep it in for five minutes before I spit it out, but it's become such a habit. I know all the health reasons why I shouldn't chew and I would like to be able to go places without carrying a bottle to spit in everywhere I'm walking.

I want to quit but I'm not sure how much my heart is in it—that's just me being truly honest. My weaknesses just go to show me that God is far from finished with me.

LESSONS LEARNED

I was pretty young when I first understood that it's tough to live at the mercy of other people's decisions. The experiences I went through with my family, growing up the way I did, led me to be more deliberate and intentional in my own life. I didn't want to repeat the same mistakes my parents made. I wanted the outcome of my life to be different, and that meant I had to make different decisions. I didn't rush into marriage, and we didn't have children until we could afford to raise them. Even something as simple as whether you force your kids to eat food they hate depends on how you were raised...and whether you want them to figure you out, like you did, how to catapult their vegetables into the gap behind the oven!

As a player, I wanted to leave a legacy for my children that they would be proud of. I wasn't nearly as concerned about statistics or awards or accolades as I was about my character. At the end of my career, when people asked whether I cheated, or whether I was malicious, or whether I played selfishly and let my teammates down, I wanted to be able to hold my head high.

I wasn't perfect as a player. I'm not perfect now. I did things I regret. But that's part of the legacy too—being accountable for what you did *and* for what you could have done better.

What defines you is how you treat people in need, whether your teammates, your family, or people in your community. Every night when I put my head on the pillow, I check if I have a clear conscience or if I need to be accountable to God and confess, "Today wasn't a good day for me. I used awful language and made a selfish decision." For me, being able to live with myself means having the humility to admit I'm not perfect and to apologize when I'm wrong. It means crying when I'm hurt, being vulnerable and open with God, myself, and my family. That's always been my heart.

During my career, people constantly told me how good I was. Living intentionally means I have to be honest and humble enough to say, "I can be better." And I'm not talking about as a ballplayer;

I'm talking about my reputation as a man, a husband, and a father. That's more important than my reputation as a pitcher could ever be. My professional career is so short compared to my life—at least I hope!—that I want to be known for being a good person.

The Hall of Fame contains its share of selfish jerks. The "hall of fame" I care about is my standing before God and my family. To be voted a hall of famer there demands an intentional life lived humbly and honestly.

Some of life's challenges come at us as hard as a 100-mile-an-hour fastball, while others are curveballs that throw us for a loop. Without God coaching me, I'd strike out swinging every time.

The emotions and attitudes that defined my childhood would have been impossible to get rid of without my faith. Anger, bitterness, and unforgiveness could have taken me right out of the game, stopping me in my tracks before I even started. Meeting Jesus as a kid got me moving forward. Knowing that *God* loved *me*, a skinny little shoeless kid in southwest Virginia, and hearing He had a plan for me, well that changed everything. As a kid, I believed with everything I had that God wanted to use me somehow.

I still believe that. In fact, that's what motivated me to write this book. I believe there's someone reading this book—maybe a bunch of someones—who need to know that they can make it. They need to know there is always a person on their side, no matter what, and it just so happens that person created the whole universe.

If I've accomplished anything, it's a testament to God. If God had a plan for me, He has a plan for everyone. If God chose to help me, He'll help you. I don't know what He has in store for you, but you can count on the fact that it's the perfect way for you to use your gifts and make a difference.

That's what God's after: difference makers and impact players. Every life is the start of a new ballgame, and all of us have got to step onto the mound or into the batter's box. Everything we go through, the "burdens" we carry, are a small price to pay for what

God chose to go through for us. The criticism and skepticism we get, whether it's being told we won't amount to anything or being told we can't achieve our dreams, that's just the world's way of dragging us down. But God knows how this is going to end up, and the open secret is that He wins.

There's a gospel song called "Wouldn't Take Nothing for my Journey Now," and the lyrics say:

"Well, I started out travelin' for the Lord many years ago,
I've had a lot of heartache; I've met a lot of grief and woe.
But when I would stumble, then I would humble down,
And there I would say I wouldn't take nothing for my journey now."

That song sums it up for me. I wouldn't trade anything I went through. God used everything in my life to make me the man I am today—and the exciting part is that His plan is just beginning. I can't wait to see what He's got up his sleeve for me next.

In a few years, a bunch of sportswriters are going to evaluate my career. They're going to paint a picture of me with numbers: How many saves did he earn? How many innings did he pitch? What was his ERA? Those sportswriters are going to decide whether or not I make it into baseball's Hall of Fame in Cooperstown, New York, along with some of the greatest players to ever play the game.

I won't lie. Going to Cooperstown would be a great honor. But I can truly say, with every ounce of honesty I've got, that if I'm never selected for that honor, I'll be okay. That's not the kind of honor that defines me. My baseball career was like spring training, and now the real game is just beginning. For the rest of my life I'm living for God's glory as a husband, a father, and a man. God knows my name, and that's all the fame I need.

EXTRAS

PHOTO ALBUM

CHILDHOOD

Billy (5) riding a hobby horse in
Marion, Virginia

Billy (6) with his sister, Chasity (4) in Grandma and Paw
Paw's front yard and our baseball field in Marion, Virginia

Billy (8) and Chasity (6) at the Lutheran Church in Marion, Virginia, where Billy's father attended

Billy (age 9 or 10) second row, second from the right. This was my recreation league team called the Twins. I didn't play too many games.

Billy (11) with Mom and Uncle Randy about to play football.
My pastor, Mike Sage, was one of the coaches. I probably
played running back.

Billy, (12) back left in dark blue sweater, with cousins Randy
(back right) and Steve (plaid shirt). We're in my Grandma
Hall's living room. That big television is where I used to
watch Braves games, Roy Rogers and WWF. They had that
TV forever!

CAPE COD, MARRIED, MINORS

Billy, 1992, Brewster White Caps, Cape Cod League. I had an absolute blast that summer and ended up on the radar of major league scouts.

Billy, 1993, Auburn, NY. My first day in professional baseball. We wore hand-me-downs from the big league club. They were the original 'rainbow' uniforms. They still had the tags in them. I wore Ken Caminiti's pants.

Billy on the mound, 1993. This was one of my abysmal starts. I either struck 'em out or walked 'em. That's my pitching coach, Tad Slowik, coming out to talk to me. Manny Acta was my first manager. He called me "Little Cowboy."

Eric Owens, Billy (center), Darren Hodges. Taken at a signing at Ferrum College in 1994, right after my first year in pro ball. Eric and I were suite mates in college. He was drafted in the fourth round by the Cincinnati Reds in 1992. Darren Hodges was drafted in 1989 or 1990 by the New York Yankees. He was working out at Ferrum when I was a student and helped me with my mechanics.

Billy and Sarah, wedding day, December 10, 1994. We were married at the Freedom Tabernacle Baptist Church in Atkins, Virginia. It was snowing outside that day. It was the most nervous I've ever been but after the ceremony I was giddy.

Billy, pitching in Double A, Jackson, Mississippi, 1995.

Billy, pitching for the Tuscon Toros, Astros Triple A, probably 1995 or 1996. I was getting ready to start. It was probably 120 degrees out there!

L-R, Randolph Hall (PawPaw), Yvonne Hall (Mom), Billy, LulaMae Hall(Grandma), 1995. Sarah and I had bought our first house in Dublin, Virginia; my mom and grandparents came to visit us.

BIG LEAGUES

Billy, 1996, classic baseball card pose. Taken in Astros spring training in Kissimmee, Florida.

Billy, 1996, Santurce, Puerto Rico. The Astros organization sent me to play winter ball for the Santurce Crabbers. They wanted me to start. While I was in Puerto Rico, Larry Dierker became the Astros manager. He came to Puerto Rico and asked me if I wanted to start. I told him, "No." And that was that.

Billy and Sarah, 1997. Taken in the tunnel outside the clubhouse at the Astrodome. We had just had our clubhouse celebration after the Houston Astros made the playoffs. I had a miserable stretch during the season; Sarah bought the cowboy hat to try to change my luck. It worked.

Pitching for the Astros in Minute Maid Park

Billy, 2004, during spring training drills, Clearwater, Florida. This was my first season with the Phillies. I loved doing spring training drills.

Billy, coming off the field with pitcher Randy Wolf, Phillies spring training, 2004, Clearwater, Florida.

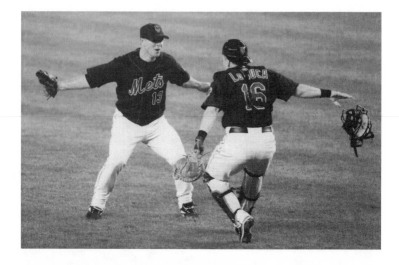

Billy and catcher Paul LoDuca, 2006. We had just clinched the 2006 Division to go to the playoffs. Paul and I were the same size so we weren't sure if I should jump in his arms or he should jump in mine. Instead we just hugged and jumped up and down. It looked pretty silly. Paul was very intense as a catcher. He was a great catcher and teammate for me.

Billy, taking the mound on opening day at Turner Field, Atlanta, Georgia, 2010. (photo by Allison Shirreffs)

BILLY WAGNER

> Drafted: Selected in the first round, 12th overall pick in 1993 by the Houston Astros

> Debut: September 13, 1995 vs. NY Mets

> Final game: October 3, 2010

> Seasons in the majors: 16

> Games: 853 games

> Innings pitched: 903

> Saves: 422, which is the second highest total for a left-handed reliever in all of baseball (John Franco is first.) It also ranks Wagner as No. 5 on the all-time saves list.

> Strikeouts: 1,196

> Lifetime ERA: 2.31

> Seven-time All Star (1999, 2001, 2003, 2005, 2007, 2008 and 2010).

> Earned the Rolaids Relief Man of Year in 1999